THE ZEN OF FUNDRAISING

Other Books by Ken Burnett

Advertising by Charities
(London: Directory of Social Change, 1984)

Charity Annual Reports
(London: Directory of Social Change, 1986)

Relationship Fundraising
(Kermarquer, France: White Lion Press, 1992)

Friends for Life
Kermarquer, France: White Lion Press, 1996)

How to Produce Inspiring Annual Reports
(with Karin Weatherup and the Burnett Works Company)
(London: Directory of Social Change, 2000)

Relationship Fundraising (2nd ed.)
(San Francisco: Jossey-Bass, 2002)

Tiny Essentials of an Effective Volunteer Board
(Kermarquer, France: White Lion Press, 2006)

THE ZEN OF FUNDRAISING

89 TIMELESS IDEAS

TO STRENGTHEN AND DEVELOP

YOUR DONOR RELATIONSHIPS

Ken Burnett

The White Lion Press

JOSSEY-BASS
A Wiley Imprint
www.josseybass.com

Published by Jossey-Bass
A Wiley Imprint
989 Market Street, San Francisco, CA 94103-1741   www.josseybass.com

Readers should be aware that Internet Web sites offered as citations and/or sources for further information may have changed or disappeared between the time this was written and when it is read.

Jossey-Bass books and products are available through most bookstores. To contact Jossey-Bass directly call our Customer Care Department within the U.S. at 800-956-7739, outside the U.S. at 317-572-3986, or fax 317-572-4002.

Jossey-Bass also publishes its books in a variety of electronic formats. Some content that appears in print may not be available in electronic books.

Credits are on page 164.

Library of Congress Cataloging-in-Publication Data

Burnett, Ken, date.
   The Zen of fundraising: 89 timeless ideas to strengthen and develop your donor relationships / Ken Burnett.
      p. cm.
   ISBN-13: 978-0-7879-8314-7 (paper)
   ISBN-10: 0-7879-8314-4 (paper)
   1. Fund raising. 2. Interpersonal communication. 3. Nonprofit organizations—Finance. I. Title.
   HG177.B876 2006
   658.15'224—dc22

                                                                    2006004497

Printed in the United States of America
FIRST EDITION
PB Printing   10 9 8 7 6 5 4 3 2 1

CONTENTS

INTRODUCTION

All You Really Need to Know About Donor Relationship Development

There's no big secret to the art and science of developing mutually rewarding relationships with donors. In essence it's all pretty much common sense. But the trouble with common sense is that too often it's not common at all. We all know that more than most commercial enterprises, nonprofit organizations will thrive only if their *customers* feel good about "doing business" with them, if their donors and other key supporters are comfortable about how they relate to the nonprofit's programs, systems, style, and people. Yet many nonprofits are embarrassingly poor at how they treat, interact with, and relate to their customers—donors and volunteers. As a result they fail to raise a lot of money that could be theirs quite easily and at little cost. Equally important, they fail to inspire and motivate many volunteers and potential supporters.

But if donor relationship development is largely a matter of common sense, experience has shown that to do it well, some things are essential, some things are important, and other things are worth knowing and worth remembering from time to time. There may be hundreds of useful *nuggets of information*, but I've selected from my experience just eighty-nine, because that's a nice convenient number and because in this book I want to concentrate solely on what's essential, rather than what's merely worth saying, or more important from your viewpoint, what's merely worth listening to. This is the first example in this book of something I call the *90-degree shift*, which I will introduce to you properly if you read on.

I can hold forth for hours, even days, perhaps months, on the endlessly fascinating subject of fundraising from donors. If I did, and if in listening to me you were to be exceptionally alert, utterly precise, and very thorough (assuming you managed to pay attention throughout), by the end of it you might—if you're really good—have made around eighty-nine separate notes summing up the most important stuff. That's what I have put into this book. The purpose of this collection is to present and describe only the things that matter most in donor relationship development, with a minimum of nonsense, bull, padding, and waffle. Please let me know whether or not you think I've succeeded.

The *Concise Oxford English Dictionary* describes *Zen* as "a form of Buddhism emphasizing the value of meditation and intuition." Zen has come to mean "thoughtful wisdom and insights." I have called this book *The Zen of Fundraising* because I hope the eighty-nine nuggets of information presented here offer you enlightenment. Some meditation upon them, backed by your intuition, should tell you if they're sound or otherwise.

In addition, sprinkled among these nuggets, you'll find thirty pieces of what's known as *twenty-first-century Zen*. These sayings are deliberate diversions, mere light relief, random thoughts to break up a succession of serious points. They shouldn't be taken too seriously. But while I hope you'll find them interesting and amusing, wise readers may discern among them some more profound meanings that are worth pondering.

Throughout this book I tend to use the phrases *donor relationship development* and *relationship fundraising* as if they were synonymous with fundraising as a whole. That shouldn't be taken as a sign that I dismiss or denigrate other forms of fundraising that do not involve or benefit from developing some sort of relationship with a donor. It's just that I'm not involved in or very interested in those forms of fundraising. And I firmly believe that if nonprofit organizations are to come close to achieving their full potential, fundraisers have to get very much better at harnessing and developing the interest, involvement, and commitment of their donors. For me, there is no valid other way. Vast potential, I am sure, will be ours if we do.

You should be aware at the outset, however, that donor relationship development is not a soft option, not something behind which you can hide a lack of fundraising success. Donor development doesn't amount to a hill of beans unless it leads to more funds raised in the long term. If it doesn't help nonprofits raise more money, it's not worth doing. I'm sure it does. In fact today the argument whether it does or not is redundant. It does. This book shows how.

The truth is, donor development is all about raising more money. It differs from the hard-sell school of fundraising in that it recognizes that because giving is voluntary, raising the maximum funds calls for rare, complex, and diverse skills and abilities, such as patience, understanding, judgment, and real commitment. Donor development is a precision tool that takes us right to the hearts of our donors, not a blunt instrument with which to bludgeon them.

That's why, although I was originally planning to call this book *Zen and the Art of Donor Development,* I readily agreed when my editor at Jossey-Bass proposed instead that we call it *The Zen of Fundraising.* For me, fundraising *is* donor development.

But there's almost nothing in this book about fundraising technique. Rather, this book concentrates on approach. It is not a how-to book, rather a book about why and why not. I'm also leaving it to others in other places to provide the empirical, statistical analysis that shows just how well relationship fundraising works. If you are still an unbeliever I recommend that you see my 1996 book, *Friends for Life: Relationship Fundraising in Practice,* or read Penelope Burk's *Donor-Centered Fundraising.*

The Zen of Fundraising opens with a summary of some of the universal problems (challenges, opportunities, or what you will) that confront fundraisers everywhere these days. As an antidote, this is followed by a list of actions I'd prioritize were I to find myself head of donor development in a progressive nonprofit. The book then describes some of the essential attitudes that all fundraisers need if they are to maximize the potential offered by their donors. The basic foundations of effective fundraising are described in detail, followed by, in turn, the keys to effectively communicating with donors, the important things to think of when relating to donors, plus the characteristics that distinguish a successful relationship fundraiser. The book ends with a look ahead to what will be important for fundraisers in the very near future.

Finally, as a Britisher writing for a U.S. publisher, I've been acutely aware that our different interpretations of the English language might cause my readers problems at times.

So I've mostly tried to put this text into American English (according to Bill Bryson, more words have now crossed the Atlantic left to right than originally crossed right to left). But inevitably, from time to time I've fallen back on a British phrase or saying that has no comfortable American equivalent. Should this cause any concern, please go to my Web site, www.whitelionpress.com, where a glossary translates idiosyncratic British terminologies. I'm sure that the troubled reader will find any elusive meaning there, and probably lots more besides.

Kermarquer, France   KEN BURNETT
January 2006

Chapter One

Playing Smart and Preparing for Action

The Trouble with Fundraising;
Plus 15 Things I'd Do If I Were the
New Head of Donor Development

I t isn't getting any easier to be a fundraiser. So it's worth considering some of the major issues and challenges facing nonprofits and the people who work for them, to try to work out how these issues and challenges might be tackled and even overcome. Here are just a few of the troubling trends and omens that are around now.

Fundraising Trends and Omens

- *Donors nowadays are much more discerning, more savvy.* They easily recognize fundraising techniques and quickly see through the schemes and devices fundraisers deploy to part them from their money. Many donors are increasingly discriminating. They search more for sincerity and commitment than for flashy, tantalizing promises. They are

1

more concerned with content than with packaging and presentation. They don't want offers; they prefer solutions. Now you don't have to be merely different; you have to be visibly distinctive.

- *Traditional fundraising methods continue to be less and less viable.* Regrettably, response to all public fundraising methods seems to decline over time, maybe in part because of the more savvy donors mentioned previously. Costs increase and effectiveness falls as the public comes to understand and see through the fundraiser's artifices and repetitiveness. Special events, nonprofit trading opportunities, direct mail, telephone fundraising, press and television advertising, face-to-face fundraising, and other forms of soliciting our publics all appear to decline in viability over time. Fundraising costs, of course, always rise.

- *Worried donors increasingly hang onto their cash.* Medical and social advances have ensured that like the rest of the population, donors now tend to be living longer. Good for them. But they are living longer in an ever more uncertain world, where state support through their declining years can be relied upon less and less and whatever wealth they have amassed may be increasingly swallowed up in providing for home and health needs through an extended old age.

- *We face a possible decline in bequest income and in major gifts too.* This decline would be a logical direct consequence of the previous observation. It has so far generally failed to materialize. But as communication becomes easier and if some of the other threats on these pages become real, this one might also. Would you agree to give a major gift or leave a legacy if you thought you might live another twenty or thirty years with inadequate pension or state support and in increasingly poor health? Among the many alarming signs of instability in today's financial markets is the increasingly heard prediction that a pension meltdown may well be coming. A bequest (legacy) meltdown could follow.

- *Resistance to fundraising direct marketing is increasing.* There's no doubt that this is happening now and posing a major threat to many fundraising programs. Most alarming is the growing body of evidence that confirms the anecdotes: most donors don't like nonprofit direct marketing. In a 1997 study among donors by Burnett Works Limited (described in the February 1998 issue of the *International Journal of Nonprofit and Voluntary Sector Marketing*), 57 percent claimed they welcome a nonprofit's newsletters, but just 2 percent said they were happy to receive fundraising direct mail. As these people are supposed to be firmly on our side, this seems to be a substantial cause for concern.

- *The hippie generation will turn out to be lousy donors.* As one of the original hippies (I still have my Joni Mitchell LPs), this is the trend I'd worry about least. But members of the hippie generation are certainly a very different kettle of fish from those of their parents' generation, and even though they may well be as generous, if not more so, they won't be as trusting or as easily convinced. With quite different moral and social values and a much healthier distrust of authority they'll probably behave very differently, so it'll pay to really understand them, that's for sure, and to deliver what they want.

- *We are putting off more donors than we inspire.* Trust and confidence in nonprofits generally may be in decline, which could be really serious. This may be the most worrying underlying factor behind the threatened decline in bequest income that I mentioned earlier. Donors discouraged by our crass communications and heavy-handed solicitations may choose to cut us out of their lives and out of their wills. Despite increased efficiency and superior marketing methodology, some statistics show that fundraising isn't growing, it's actually in decline. Notwithstanding successes at individual nonprofits, in the UK the number of households giving to charities apparently dropped for several successive years recently. It may be on the rise again, but that's from a fairly low base. And for how long?

- *Too many fundraisers are chasing too few donors.* No mistaking this danger. There are ever more fundraisers asking and list building these days, and the segment of society known as donors is hardly growing at all. Some donors feel they're being hit by fundraisers just a little too hard and a lot too often. Fundraisers constantly expend energy, funds, and credibility trying to expand their market into younger audiences. Yet all return eventually to fish in the same well-defined pond, the one where most donors are fifty-plus, middle class, well educated, and with disposable incomes— a finite pond indeed.

- *Public alarm at the cost of fundraising is evident.* This concern is increasingly justified, as some of our statistics are now all but indefensible. But mostly, we fundraisers are prudent stewards of the funds our publics trust to us. Given a fair hearing we can generally offer convincing explanations that will assuage any alarm. Trouble is, our public's attention span is often nowhere near enough to allow anything other than a superficial look at our statistics, and the

4

top-line figures are often not sufficiently encouraging. So the alarm escalates. Well aware of the public's relish for copy that knocks nonprofits, the media are constantly on the lookout for any hints of impropriety from fundraisers. Media interest, and the incidence of shabby reporting that inevitably follows, seems likely to grow.

- *Donors resent the big business appearance of many nonprofits.* So they will increasingly turn to the nontraditional types of giving that are springing up everywhere, such as those available through DonorsChoose (www.donorschoose.org) and GlobalGiving (www.globalgiving.com). This may be no bad thing, but it's a new kind of competition that should worry the hell out of those big fundraisers that act like corporations.

- *New legislation is being passed to protect donors and control fundraisers.* This threat pops up increasingly in most countries where fundraising is developed. Some of this legislation is good and desirable. But often these new laws are drawn up by people with scant knowledge of fundraising and fundraisers, and the nonprofit sector learns too late that effective, donor-centered self-regulation would have been much better.

- *Finding new donors is becoming unacceptably expensive.* Fundraisers frequently say their acquisition cost is now so high it's barely viable to recruit new donors, which signals a serious dilemma for the future. Put another way, many nonprofits report that donor recruitment is now too expensive, so instead they are turning to donor development. This is perhaps a wise thing to do if it signifies an end to the days of *churn and burn.* But cutting acquisition is real short-term thinking from an organizational health perspective. It's equivalent to eating your seed corn.

- *Soon it'll be a simple matter for donors to cut fundraisers out of their lives entirely.* Donors in future will expect most of the communications they receive to come into their homes via their telephone line or whatever electronic process will replace telephone lines in the near future. So all unwanted communications could be screened out easily. And finally . . .

- *Short-term gain equals long-term suicide.* This is shorthand for the nigh-universal phenomenon that fundraisers today tend to concentrate on short-term issues and income, often at the expense of laying lasting foundations for their fund-raising, so doing long-term damage to the causes that they claim to serve. *Short-termism* is a major problem for today's fundraisers. In the pursuit of short-term gains, here-today-gone-tomorrow fundraisers inflict lasting damage on their organizations' future fundraising prospects.

At first glance these trends and omens might seem daunting, even depressing. Yet, with sound strategies for effective donor relationship development, it seems to me that the future is not all doom and gloom, far from it. By focusing on building more mutually beneficial relationships with our donors, we fundraisers can turn all these negative trends around. There's evidence, and lots of it, from fundraisers in several countries, that donor-centered relationship fundraising can and does transform fundraising results. In fact, if you can get right the thinking and the attitudes that underpin successful fundraising, there's probably never been a better time to be a fundraiser.

As an antidote to some of the anxieties just listed, here's what I would do now if I were starting out again as manager of a fundraising department. The fifteen strategies that follow should, in my view, form the core of the fundraising department of the future.

What I Would Do If I Were
the New Head of Donor Development

I don't expect you, my reader, to instantly implement all the eighty-nine tips and nuggets of advice that follow in these chapters and that form the main purpose of this book, though it would be nice if you did. But if you're starting out in donor development and want to know what to focus on as priorities, the following short list of fifteen points may help you.

If at first you don't succeed . . . skydiving is not for you.

This list came about when a U.S. journal for fundraisers asked me to imagine I'd just started in a new job, with a clean slate and sufficient resources to set about transforming the donor development function. I include it here to help anyone in an even vaguely similar situation—and to help me set out early in this book my philosophy of donor development.

These fifteen strategies aren't the only things I'd do. They may not even be the most urgent things I'd do or even the most important. But they are the things I'd do that I think would have the most lasting impact, that would make the most difference to converting my imaginary donor development department from the underfunded, misunderstood appendage to the fundraising function that I found on joining the organization into the finely honed, high-earning core activity that I'd like to leave behind me when, in the fullness of time, I move on to pastures new (you have to indulge me a little here in this fantasy).

1
I'd aspire to be the most learned fundraiser of my generation.

Apart from studying the lessons of history and going to the best seminars and workshops, for the fundraising resource center that I'd set about creating I'd (at the very least) get hold of the ten best books on fundraising (see point 78, in Chapter Seven). And I'd make sure these books don't gather dust on the resource center's shelves but are really used. Plus I'd subscribe to the best trade magazines and journals around. And I'd encourage each of my colleagues to set aside half an hour each day (of their own time, preferably) for *essential fundraising reading*. I'd challenge each of them every day to try to get at least one new idea from this, an idea that would help keep us just a bit ahead of everyone else who's clamoring for our donors' funds. And once each month at least, I'd encourage them to visit a fundraising organization with which they've had no prior contact whatsoever. Or to call a fundraiser for advice, someone they've never spoken to before.

I could also suggest that, each day, they wave at someone they don't know. But that may be going too far.

2
I'd teach all my fundraising colleagues to make the 90-degree shift and to aspire to be fifteen minutes ahead.

These two fundamental attitudes underpin the best approach to donor development and are explained in detail in points 22 and 23 (in Chapter Two).

The first attitude, making the 90-degree shift, will involve putting all of us in the department firmly in our donors' shoes, seeing everything the organization does through our donors' eyes. It sounds uncomfortable and it's not easy, but nothing else will come as close to helping us build mutually beneficial relationships with our donors. Imagine—instead of giving donors what we want them to have, when we make the 90-degree shift we can be sure to offer them only what they want to receive!

The second attitude, aspiring to be fifteen minutes ahead, means I would concentrate not on finding those rare, elusive big breakthrough ideas to advance our fundraising; instead I'd focus on implementing the myriad small but cumulatively significant ideas that are all around fundraisers today, waiting to be picked up. There are eighty-nine of these ideas in this little book—more than that for the thoughtful reader.

For I know that's how our fundraising is most likely to move fastest, not in a few risky giant steps but in lots of sensible, even obvious, but demonstrably sound little ones.

Before focusing in any detail on the techniques and skills that fundraisers need, I'd make sure my own thinking was right, and I'd encourage my colleagues to get their thinking right too. Before I'd unleash any of my well-meaning fundraising colleagues on our poor, unsuspecting donors who deserve so much better than they usually get, I'd ensure that these colleagues start off with all the good habits fundraisers need to acquire. So I'd rigorously remind them of the basic foundations of our profession, the essential values and approaches that underpin good fundraising. To help, I'd make sure they have all read and understood Chapters Two and

Three of this book. I wouldn't let them even talk to a donor until they'd passed muster on the basics.

3
I'd develop a culture of appropriate but high-quality donor service in our organization, top to bottom.

I'd make sure our organization is always a pleasure to do business with. Tragically, nonprofits are not very good at customer service and that is an understatement. All fundraisers should perhaps reflect that customer service is like personal hygiene— without it, your relationships won't even get started.

Not a savory thought, I'm sure you'll agree. Yet experience tells me good, appropriate customer service is missing in most of my competitors (so providing it is just one more way my organization will be fifteen minutes ahead). As almost every mystery shopping test confirms, fundraisers are almost invariably rotten at customer service. In the past most donors haven't expected anything better, but as customer expectations rise generally, that will change for nonprofits for sure. To enhance the experience of being a donor to our nonprofit, everyone in my department will offer the most appropriate, most friendly, most efficient, and most effective customer service to be found anywhere. All at a time that suits our donors rather than suits us. So our donors will like doing business with us. And they'll tell their friends.

I'd get all my fundraisers used to saying thank you and you're welcome promptly and properly. Our organization would be a nice place to be and to be in contact with. (See points 62 to 65, in Chapter Five, for more specific advice on effective, appropriate customer service — one of the easiest and best ways to get fifteen minutes ahead.)

TO PROVE THE POINT: THE MYSTERY ABOUT MYSTERY SHOPPING TESTS IS WHY WE FUNDRAISERS SEEM UNABLE TO LEARN FROM THEM

So-called mystery shopping tests provide easy, cheap copy for magazine editors, so our trade press is full of them. They always present the same depressing story, illustrating how deficient nonprofits are in providing even basic standards of customer service, while hinting at what this might be costing these organizations in lost opportunities and disappointed donors. But the self-flagellation that should accompany the reading of these indictments can't have much effect because these magazines never report improvement.

A Sydney-based agency, Pareto Fundraising, has just reported on the first in what's intended to be an annual series of mystery tests (www.paretofundrasing.com). The agency's aim is to *benchmark* customer service levels from nearly one hundred nonprofits in Australia and New Zealand, comparing results to those obtained among similar nonprofits in the UK. Predictably, none of the three countries excelled this time, though the colonials did noticeably better than those in mother England. How would North American nonprofits fare in similar tests, one wonders? Having mystery tested in both the United States and Canada in the past, I'm maintaining diplomatic silence.

11

But the test results aren't likely to be good.

This Australian study assessed nonprofit responses by phone, mail, and e-mail to four specific opportunities: a donor making a one-time credit card gift, a donor setting up a regular monthly gift, a donor asking for specific information, and a donor inquiring about how to leave a bequest. Lack of space precludes giving the full results, but the following should give you food for thought.

- The level of failure to respond was incomprehensibly high across all tests. Up to 20 percent of nonprofits don't respond when approached by someone trying to give them money.
- Nearly half of nonprofits don't promote regular giving to someone who has given a one-time gift.
- Up to 40 percent don't formally thank donors when they set up a regular gift.
- It's not unusual for nonprofits to take weeks, even months, to respond to a simple request.
- Five nonprofits that sent receipts or confirmations never actually took the donation from the credit card.
- Nonprofits perform very poorly when asked about bequests. Of those that replied to the suggestion that a donor might wish to leave them a bequest, only 22 percent said thank you, and just 36 percent explained the difference between pecuniary and residuary bequests. A full 31 percent didn't respond at all.

Though their sample sizes are often not statistically valid and their methodology is sometimes suspect, in general such tests show response times are poor, too many organizations don't respond at all, and many nonprofits fail to deliver what they promise, fail in basic politeness and accountability, and miss opportunities to promote themselves. Their processing systems are inefficient, and there is a conspicuous failure to listen to supporters. In all, good opportunities exist for the surveyed organizations to pull their socks up for next year's tests, or for other nonprofits to move fifteen minutes ahead.

Or are we really incapable of learning from this kind of thing?

4
I'd be very choosy.

Fundraisers almost never have unlimited resources, so of necessity we have to be choosy. Nowadays, we need to be very selective in where we focus our attention. So I'd concentrate my department's resources finely. My colleagues and I wouldn't be able to build relationships with everyone, so we'd focus our energies and resources on those who really count. Remember, real donors are rare creatures. A real donor is someone who has shown a propensity to support your cause over time. People who have given just once, in my definition, are responders, not yet donors. So we'd aspire to ask fewer people for more money for better reasons. We'd set out to find the real donors, because we know real profit comes from real relationships with real donors.

5
I'd cut out all short-term thinking, including all hard-sell activities.

Instead, my department would lay solid foundations for a secure and lasting future that's not driven by short-term targets or objectives. I'd start by searching out opportunities for mutual benefit. I'd lay down strategies to develop committed giving and bequest income. I'd banish all high-pressure activities and make sure that my colleagues and I didn't sell to our donors; instead we would work with them and for them, as respected counselors and friends.

Before criticizing someone you should walk a mile in their shoes . . . then you're a mile away, and you have their shoes.

Fundraisers should put an end to the hard sell, lay foundations for the future, and invest in and plan for the long term. The long-term nature of most fundraising should be made clear to all fundraisers when they join an organization.

6
I'd switch our organization's contact paradigm from *marketing* to *communication*.

Donors don't like to be sold to. They never did. Effective communications, we are reliably informed by research, build trust and confidence among our donors. And trust and confidence are the foundations of good relationship development. I'd make communication with donors a dialogue, not a monologue. I'd recruit to my team genuine expertise and a track record in effective communication. Our nonprofit's story would get told. And how!

I'd foster the lost art of storytelling and practice *experience fundraising* (see points 37, in Chapter Three, and 80, in Chapter Seven).

Fundraising isn't about asking for money. It's about inspiring people to believe that they can make a difference — then helping them to make it. So fundraising is the inspiration business, and however much we may try to elevate and complicate it, at its heart it is little more than telling stories. I'd encourage all my fellow fundraisers to become master storytellers. Most of the time our donors can't be where the organization's work is, to see for themselves the good work our organization does. So we fundraisers need to be able to take them there in words and pictures, to paint images of our work so successfully in their minds that it will be like the donor is almost there in person, experiencing it for himself or herself.

7
I'd make sure my nonprofit sends only effective, imaginative communications.

The problem with most nonprofit communications is that they are dull. Given the abundance of colorful, dramatic human interest material with which nonprofits are blessed, this is a shocking admission. Yet sadly it's true. Fundraisers are prolific producers of printed and electronic communications, but the bulk of them are tedious, vacuous, or fit only for the trash can — sometimes all three. Common weaknesses are using too many words, failing to design for readability, and emphasizing what the organization wants to say rather than what the reader wants to read. If you think this a little harsh, send off for the newsletters or annual reports of, say, twenty prominent nonprofits and see if I'm wrong (see point 63, in Chapter Five, for ideas about comparing your nonprofit to others).

You can't write effectively without also seeing the reader, in your mind's eye at least. Communication is a bit like kissing. It takes two to do it properly.

You should send only communications that will help ensure your supporters

- Are entirely comfortable
- Will grow in their trust and confidence in you and your organization
- Actually look forward to hearing from you
- Hear only about issues and subjects that truly interest them
- Give when you ask
- Feel they are benefiting from the relationship too

It's important that fundraisers become more self-critical of what they produce so they send only creative and effective communications, and that they save the money currently being wasted on inappropriate and poorly constructed publications by not sending them, thus avoiding inflicting unhelpful, unwelcome materials on their dear donors.

- Constantly measure donors' interest in and reactions to what they receive from you. Learn from this.
- Ask yourself whether or not your donors actually read what you send them.
- Never be dull, bland, or unmoving. Communicate with passion. We have the best stories in the world to tell, and the best reasons for telling them.
- Invest in good pictures and in people who can write compellingly, with power and passion.

- Design for readability (see point 55, in Chapter Four).
- Send less but better. Make sure what goes to donors is only the truly excellent.

For more on good communication, see Chapter Four.

TO PROVE THE POINT: FUNDRAISING AS MOOSE SPIT SOAP

Too often fundraising products just don't do "what it says on the wrapper." We fundraisers promise, but we don't deliver. We raise expectations, then we disappoint. Because people are very tolerant of nonprofits, we get away with this for a while. But not forever.

In Canada recently I came across a weird product called Moose Spit Soap. In fact it was labeled "Authentic Wilderness Moose Spit Soap." I was impressed, and as I'd been searching for something authentic and useful (and not too expensive) as gifts for my family and friends, I was on the point of buying several bars.

Imagine my dismay then, when on closer reading of the small print I discerned the legend, "There is no actual moose spit in this soap."

"What," I found myself wondering aloud, "is Moose Spit Soap if it doesn't contain any actual moose spit?"

The answer is simple. It's just plain soap. Too often, that's fundraising. Just plain soap.

8
I'd make my department a listening and a hearing organization.

In addition to training myself and my fundraising colleagues in how to provide appropriate yet highly professional levels of service and donor care, I'd make sure we know what our donors want and that we implement what they want us to do. I'd meet and talk to donors at every opportunity. I'd offer our donors a say in formulating our strategies; I'd encourage feedback, comments, questions, and complaints; I'd regularly research current donors' views (and those of former donors too); and I'd survey and measure donor satisfaction. I'd keep simple indices of these findings, which in time would become key performance indicators (KPIs) or even KDIs (key donor indicators), the regular data I'd use to monitor and report on fundraising performance. I know I'd be ahead in this, because most fundraisers measure their performance only in terms of money received now. (Also see point 66, in Chapter Five.)

In all their communications fundraisers need to switch from monologue to dialogue. In addition to investing effort and resources into knowing and understanding their donors, they should make sure donors don't adopt a passive role but instead can readily become active participants who will get as involved as possible (within their own levels of comfort). This can be achieved by offering donors genuinely interesting and worthwhile involvement opportunities, inviting donors to visit and see your work for themselves, so they really can get under your organization's skin and become not just participants but co-owners of your cause. To achieve this, your organization has to become a listening and hearing organization.

There are six keys to becoming a listening and hearing organization:

- Train frontline personnel.
- Involve donors strategically.
- Encourage feedback, comments, questions, even complaints.
- Undertake regular research—listen particularly to donors and to former supporters.
- Regularly survey donor satisfaction—monitor and report on key indices.
- Don't just listen—really hear what your donors will tell you, and act on what you learn.

If we've been put on this earth to help others . . . what are the others here for?

9
I'd work on strategies that build our donors' trust and confidence in us; I'd make our nonprofit a model of proactive accountability, to show it is effective and well run.

This means that in addition to producing the best, most involving, and most welcome communications in all practical formats, my colleagues and I would try to make our communications into models of good stewardship. I'd publish "The Standards We Set Ourselves" in our annual report. I'd offer donors a charter that sets out clearly our organization's commitment to them, explaining how it proposes to be an excellent steward of the funds they entrust to its care. I'd get these communications to volunteers and other key supporters and constituents too.

Transparent accountability isn't just a duty, it's an opportunity. Demonstrable good governance and open, proactive accountability will be hallmarks of the successful fundraising organization of the future. Increasingly donors expect nonprofits to be fully accountable, and they will come to demand ever more evidence of efficient and effective governance. But it will pay if you don't wait for donors to ask. Demonstrate your good stewardship and commitment to full accountability at every opportunity. Invite and encourage comment and questions. That alone will reassure donors.

The impact of good governance on fundraising can be profound, and it will grow in the future. I'd recommend to my colleagues that they read about the essentials of good governance in such books as Kay Sprinkel Grace's *Over Goal!* (Emerson and Church, 2003) and in my own book on the subject, *Tiny Essentials of an Effective Volunteer Board* (White Lion Press, 2006).

Fundraisers have to champion accountability and take it to their donors. As explained earlier the media are always happy to exploit any hint of poor management or inefficiency from nonprofits, and the public are only too prepared to follow where journalists lead. Yet fundraisers usually have nothing to hide and lots to be proud of. Generally nonprofits do a lot better than the public thinks they do. We need to illustrate our effectiveness and efficiency clearly and to strongly champion these qualities, rather than trying to keep our heads down and hoping questions will just go away. So I'd tell the others in my department:

- Invite donors to ask questions. Make it easy for them.
- Show your donors their file. Offer your donors on-line access to their account and to any other information you hold on them.
- Promote your organization as financially prudent and well run (make sure first that it is). Invite donors to come and see for themselves.
- Make available to those donors that wish to have them the details of your financial systems, risk and impact assessment procedures, and other techniques and systems of good governance. Circulate key audiences (staff, volunteers, and donors who ask for them) with details of what happens at your board meetings, including full minutes (editing out anything of a genuinely sensitive or confidential nature, such as a disciplinary procedure). Many organizations now post highlights of board meetings on their intranet or Web site. Donors, I am sure, will approve.

10
I'd focus on the major motivations that have attracted donors to our organization's cause in the first place; I'd try to understand these motivations and make the best possible use of them.

Donors to one organization will often exhibit a varied range of motivations, differing not just from donors to other causes but from other donors to the same cause. After I had identified all the main motivations that apply in my organization, I'd make sure everyone else knows about them too. Then I'd build strategies addressing these motivations and blend them

21

into our future communications. For example, a nonprofit serving children with a disability may have donors who are there because they have a professional connection, they feel sympathy or pity for the children, they have a family member with this condition, or they are angry that more isn't being done, and so on. Creatively addressing these fundamental yet very different and distinctive motivations will ensure our organization's donors get more from their support of our cause. When this happens, I'm confident our fundraising results will rocket.

11
I'd have my nonprofit's donor database properly profiled at least once each year.

We need to know our donor file inside out so we can make sure we have the most useful information on our donors, what they are doing, and what they are thinking. This information has to be available to us at all times and in ways we can easily access. Very often organizations have lots of information on their donors but don't know how to access it or what to do with it, such as calculating *lifetime giving* (LTG—a donor's giving total to date) and *lifetime value* (LTV—what a donor will give you in his or her lifetime). In my organization, my colleagues and I would use this process to identify the real donors hidden within our file, so we could aim to ask fewer people for more money for better reasons. We would then combine this empirical information with all the other research data we have gathered (see point 8, in this chapter) to ensure that we are doing all we can to optimize and grow all our donors' lifetime values.

12
I'd offer donors and other supporters the chance to choose when and how often they hear from us and what they might want to hear about.

Which do you think will work best? If we send our donors what we want them to have or if we send what they are willing and happy, or at least prepared, to receive? It's the 90-degree shift again. Donors will always be more responsive when what we send them is what they want to receive.

My colleagues and I would aspire to send donors only what interests them and what they're most likely to respond to. Giving our donors the right choices would enable us to segment our donor file not just by the two traditional levels of segmentation, demographic characteristics and past behavior, but by choice, a third level. We would continually ask our donors what they want and do our best to deliver it.

Giving customers choices has become known as *permission marketing*. A few far-sighted nonprofits have been practicing it for years and getting exceptional results. Nowhere is permission marketing more appropriate than for nonprofit fundraisers.

My colleagues and I would let our approach to fundraising communication be driven by what interests and involves our donors. Giving donors choices is a perfect example of the 90-degree shift. Having made our organization and its offerings as interesting, appropriate, and involving as possible, I'd be confident that our donors would safely and reliably choose for themselves the level of closeness and the content that would most suit their interest in and capacity for involvement with our cause.

When this strategy starts to work I'll try introducing other choices for our donors, so they can in effect choose their own personal communications programs. I know the technology that makes this possible is getting better and cheaper all the time. And I know donors give much more regularly and more happily when they feel their wishes are taken into account. So this is another area where I'll be able to be fifteen minutes ahead.

Then, with this and all the other learnings I've gathered from the points in this chapter, I'd structure a fundraising strategy that employs the best of current techniques and practices, focusing on fundraising that motivates rather than discourages our donors.

13
I'd create an environment where innovation and creativity can flourish, so I could readily develop appropriate products and propositions designed to suit our donors.

It pays to offer donors appropriate products they will want to buy. These days, if a nonprofit hasn't got monthly giving, high-value donor (HVD), and legacy products, then it is already behind. Product design and development is a sophisticated field for fundraisers. Most new products fail, and that's as true in the nonprofit world as commercially. But that should never deter fundraisers from investing appropriately in new product development or from learning and borrowing from the experience of others. A vast body of knowledge and experience has now been built up of what works and what doesn't in fundraising, so this is a good area for creative plagiarism, for borrowing the best of what works for others.

Yet in the world our donors inhabit, lazy, look-alike fundraising abounds. Somewhere in the mists of time (or more likely, at a succession of quite recent fundraising seminars) we fundraisers were taught and came to accept that there are fixed formulas to guide us, that to get the best responses we must slavishly follow the "right" procedures, that to obtain maximum savings and optimum returns our communications have to fit a limited range of standard shapes, styles, and sizes, that what works for one organization will surely also work for another.

They were right, those teachers who propounded these wisdoms. (Though I suspect that many of the fundraising gurus who teach at seminars and workshops also own direct marketing and communications businesses that thrive when fundraisers all blindly follow the conventions of their trades.) Nevertheless, fundraisers all want to minimize costs and maximize returns, so through the processes of testing and plagiarizing we have all wound up copying pretty much what everyone else does. The result for our poor donors (and even our rich donors) is that they wind up getting piles and piles of requests that all look pretty much the same. Yet we know that the beginning of success is to be different; the beginning of failure is to be the same.

On average our donors are quite intelligent people. Ere long they begin to see through our techniques, which are generally pretty transparent, not to say often ham-fisted. Who was it that first imagined donors would be fooled for long by letters that start with that moronic salutation "Dear Friend"?

(OK, Dr. Thomas Barnardo, I have to suppose, whom I mention in point 25 [in Chapter Two]. But I guess even he'd be astounded to find that nearly 120 years after he coined this bland generalization we still trot it out daily, as if there were no permitted alternative. Are we sheep, or what?)

So maybe it isn't sensible any longer to have mailings that look so obviously mass produced, with envelopes with addresses that show through windows or with prepaid bulk postage imprints and carrying letters with lots of short paragraphs, underlining, and indenting and inevitably all ending with at least one postscript (better known as the PS). We should acknowledge now that the majority of our donors and potential donors are perceptive enough to see through such artifice.

From any viewpoint, nonprofit organizations constantly need to be reviewing the products and propositions they offer donors, even if it's just the continuing efficacy or otherwise of the basic proposition "give us your money."

There's ample evidence around to show that those organizations that have embraced R&D, as it might be called in corporate businesses, and offered their donors appropriate new products and propositions have prospered disproportionately. Think of child and animal sponsorship, monthly donor schemes, bequest giving clubs, and so on.

Think too of the prizes that might come to those who do things differently, who innovate, who stand out from the herd . . . and not just in format (it's often quite hard to break from the conventions that have been imposed upon us). We can also be imaginative in offer and in audience and always in how we present our message, in our creative treatment, and in how we tell our stories.

No doubt, in fundraising it pays to be first, as I'm sure fundraisers down the ages have known well. But it also pays to move on. Those organizations that first experimented in off-the-page advertising did spectacularly well in Britain in the 1950s and '60s. The pioneers of direct-mail fundraising in the United States and the UK during the 1970s and '80s built massive donor lists that are now the greatest of assets for these far-sighted fundraisers. Those first in telephone fundraising cleaned up, whereas the entrepreneurs who gave us direct dialogue, better known in most of the world as face-to-face fundraising, very quickly and cost effectively recruited hundreds of thousands of regular monthly donors and raised millions of dollars, pounds, or euros for the causes they represent. Those in the vanguard of the new communications revolution (see point 58, in Chapter Four) will most probably reap similar benefit.

Undeniably, spectacularly glittering prizes await successful innovators in fundraising. But fundraisers also are a cautious lot and adequate budgets for research and development are not often to be found in the nonprofit world. This won't do. Fundraisers have to innovate fearlessly and constantly. More alarming is the culture of *heads down* that pervades, the fear of being different, and the almost irresistible compulsion to be the same.

Given the urgency of our causes, such conservatism is unforgivable. We should reject totally a culture of caution and instead build for ourselves environments that are in constant turmoil, where change and invention are nurtured and encouraged, where innovation is honored, even revered, and where *wrong* is not necessarily a bad place to be. This may require a new approach to budgeting. The innovation culture's understanding of failure is totally different from that of the operation's culture. In the innovation culture each failure takes us a step closer to ultimate success. Donors need to understand this and to be a part of it. (They often are—and enthusiastically so. In America these generous, rich, and far-sighted people are referred to as *entrepreneurial donors*, or even *philanthrepreneurs*. Maybe that is going a bit too far. . . .)

I'm not suggesting we sink all our resources into the search for innovation. Ten or even 5 percent of net income would do. Actually, for most organizations even 1 percent would be nice. Provided that along with the cash would come a commitment to change current organizational thinking and to elevate innovation and all that goes with it to its proper place. If it's really committed to be the best in this area, the serious non-profit will regularly review the people in charge of the innovation process and determine how well it encourages staff to collaborate on product and service improvements, generates and captures new ideas, bounces back after a wrong decision, and measures up to competitors and their innovations. This is not an area for the faint-hearted. (See also my connected comments on risk taking in point 75, in Chapter Six.)

TO PROVE THE POINT:
THE DELIGHT OF
DOING WITHOUT

Although I'm an eager advocate of positive change and appropriate innovation, I have to confess I'm a little disillusioned with the so-called technological advances of recent years. Perhaps the real wonder of modern gadgetry and gimmickry is how good you feel when you do without them. This reminds me of the story of the rabbi and the poor man who lived in one small room with his wife and three children.

"I can't stand it!" wailed the man. "What can I do?" The rabbi told him to get a dog. The dog barked at the children and messed up the floor. Then the rabbi suggested he get some hens. The dog chased the hens, which frightened the baby. "Get a goat," insisted the rabbi. And so on, until the rabbi added a horse, and the whole thing became completely impossible. "Now, get rid of them all," said the rabbi, "and tell me how you feel." "It's wonderful!" cried the man in gratitude. "There's just me and the wife and the children, and we have the whole room to ourselves."

Possibly the gadget we really need is the one that we can program to get rid of all the others.

All progress may indeed be in the hands of unreasonable people, but it seems to me that the rest of us should reserve a healthy skepticism for all changes and supposed advances. I'll underline this point by quoting, from a perhaps unlikely source, an argument that questions the basis of our enthusiasm for change and innovation:

> "Advances—what advances? The number of hours women devote to housework has not changed since 1930, despite all the vacuum cleaners, washers, dryers, trash compactors, garbage disposals, wash-and-wear fabrics. Why does it still take as long to clean the house as it did in 1930?
>
> "It's because there haven't been any advances. Yet 30,000 years ago when men were doing cave paintings at Lascaux, they worked just 20 hours a

week and the rest of the time they could play, or
sleep, or do whatever they wanted" [mathematician
Ian Malcolm, a character in Michael Crichton's
Jurassic Park].

Evidence perhaps that in reality we have made no progress
whatsoever. But I suspect that 30,000 years ago, while
the men had all that time to play, sleep, or whatever, the
women still had to spend just as long doing the housework.
Plus ça change . . .

14
I'd make our organization
the best communicator anywhere.

Effective communication is so important for fundraisers I've
devoted a whole chapter to it in this book (see Chapter Five).
So as the new head of our fundraising department I'd study
thoroughly the ever-increasing and improving options for the
new customer relationship manage-
ment (CRM) technology that's just
around the corner for fundraisers. At
the right time for our organization,
I'd invest prudently in it. These new
communications systems (which in
the future may not be called CRM
because of the negative associations

We don't stop
playing because
we grow old . . . we
grow old because
we stop playing.

that often surround that term) will transform the way fundraisers deal with donors, just as the development of electronic databases transformed fundraising potential twenty years or so ago.
But I'd hope not to forget that this leap forward will have less

to do with technology, more to do with processes, and much more to do with people. When installing donor databases some years back, many fundraising organizations got it badly and expensively wrong (for a variety of generally not very good reasons, largely to do with a failure to anticipate needs properly and a reluctance to invest sufficiently). My colleagues and I would have a chance now to learn from the past and so get it right this time. We'd take the decision carefully and thoroughly of course. But I'd make sure we took it bravely, so that our organization could stay that all-important fifteen minutes ahead. And so we could treat our donors exactly as we'd wish to be treated ourselves.

15
Finally, I'd give a little bit extra.

To stand out you have to be outstanding. So in fundraising it pays to go further than expected. My colleagues and I, therefore, would always offer a bonus, particularly but not exclusively when dealing with donors one-to-one. We'd have competitions to see who could come up with the most cost-effective and original extra mile that we could go for our donors.

TO PROVE THE POINT:
WHERE RADICAL, ADVENTUROUS,
YET THOROUGH GIVING
BECOMES NORMAL

A new phenomenon is springing up in villages, towns, and cities across the land, heralding the arrival of a new kind of donor brought in and sustained by a new format and even a new kind of giving.

This innovation is known as the *giving group,* sometimes also called a *giving club* or a *giving circle.* There are few rules and prerequisites. A giving group is set up when neighbors, colleagues, friends, or whoever get together to form themselves into a donating entity so they can more easily choose, monitor, and maintain their giving. Usually, members of giving groups are anxious to ensure that their giving is appropriate and effective, so their combined strength as a group ensures a demanding and thorough but potentially very dedicated and loyal supporter. These groups are looking for fundraisers prepared to routinely go the extra mile to give them what they want. But they will make it very worth the fundraiser's while.

One group of my acquaintance includes my friend and colleague John Grain, a professional fundraiser with seventeen years' experience, now working as director of stewardship with the Cascaid Group in Reading, UK. John recently asked each of the members of his group to list the major reasons why he or she is a donor. They came up with eight, in no particular order.

I want to be recognized and valued for my gift.

I want to feel good about giving.

I want to know how my money will be used and what difference it will make.

I want to be inspired.

I want to feel involved, a part of something.

I want to be impressed, so I can tell others about the cause and recruit them to support it.

I want you to ask my opinion.

I want to know that you listen to me.

Providing imaginative answers to these needs is the way forward for fundraisers. John's group will be asking all the organizations to which they donate to meet these donor interests. Group members will expect prompt and appropriate acknowledgments and thank-yous; great newsletters and reports; swift and relevant feedback; the chance to supply input, to be asked and listened to; proactive accountability; invitations to events and projects; and the opportunity to see for themselves the impact of their giving.

I venture to suggest that before long John's group will become a very good donor: rigorous, supportive, and tolerant but ultimately uncompromising. If fundraisers for the causes the group chooses don't deliver, they won't get the group's support, at least not for long. This, I think, will be a very, very good thing.

Chapter Two

RIGHT FROM THE START

10 Concepts That Will Ensure Your Thinking Is Sound

Without doubt, if you are to excel at fundraising and, particularly, in the art of donor relationship development, the first thing you must do is get your thinking right. To help you do this, I have found several specific attitudes of mind to be important. They are worth describing in some detail. And so you don't think it's all plain sailing, at the end of this chapter I've also included five cautions worth heeding.

16
Give your donors what they want.

We'll succeed only when we stop concentrating on what we, the fundraisers, want and instead start delivering what they, our donors, want. This statement is merely simple sense, but we so often don't do it, or do it badly.

Simple it may be, but more than any other thing, changing our approach in this way would transform our fundraising performance. It seems appropriate that what in practice is the most elusive key to fundraising success is also the most obvious. If we wish to develop strong, mutually beneficial, lasting relationships with donors we have to deliver what they want, when they want it, in the way they want it. Usually this will coincide with what we want too, or we can make it coincide with what we want. But first and foremost we must deliver what *they* want. This process is sometimes called being *donor-focused* or *donor-led*. I call it *relationship fundraising,* because it involves developing an individual and appropriate relationship with each willing donor, one where the donor feels comfortably in control and can tell you how she or he would like the relationship to develop. That relationship might be very close or so remote as to be negligible. The important thing is that it should be what the donor wants. Each donor will have a specific idea of how he or she wishes to be treated, somewhere between neglect and overkill. The fundraiser's challenge is to identify where on that spectrum each individual donor's comfort level is to be found.

We have to deliver what our donors want consistently so their role as a donor gives them pleasure and satisfaction and doesn't make them feel pressured, troubled, or inconvenienced. If you have determined to be a fundraiser, I recommend that each day you acknowledge that being a donor is ideally something people do entirely voluntarily. If they feel coerced into it, they won't stay donors for long. It's something they choose to do, often in spite of rather than because of a professional fundraiser. Our job is to help them to get more from the process. We have to have an amount of faith to believe this approach will pay, not always perhaps in the short term but at least in the medium and long term. After nearly three decades as a fundraiser, I'm convinced of it.

17
Really understand your donors.

If you want your donors to understand you, you must first understand them. In-depth understanding of your donors is not an option; it's crucial for survival as much as for success. Nonprofits generally underinvest in the many devices and techniques they might employ to really understand their donors so they can get ever better at supplying what each donor wants (the main secret of success).

Traditionally fundraisers have been very slow to realize the importance of good market knowledge and to appreciate that if they are really to understand their donors they have no other option than to invest sensibly in sustained, relevant research. In making this often spectacularly false economy they have condemned themselves to live as permanent victims of the curse of assumptions, wrongly anticipating their donors' true feelings and emotions because they simply didn't know any better.

Recently though there's been an explosion in research studies, both practical and academic. Now fundraisers face a different problem: knowing the difference between what in this research is *really important*, that which they cannot be without; what is nice to know but not essential; and what is, frankly, not worth bothering with. This last category probably accounts for the largest part of what's now around, and although the other two categories are growing fast, it's growing fastest. Knowing what you don't need is becoming just as useful as knowing what you need.

Lack of understanding of our donors comes at a price. With the exception perhaps of a small number of major donors who obviously justify special treatment, fundraisers have for generations tended to treat all their donors as if they are the same. Economic necessity has certainly been a big factor in this but so has the fact that we really haven't understood what makes each donor different. Imagine what a breakthrough it would be if we could understand (and so address) the main motivations behind our donors' different decisions to give . . .

Understanding the many distinct motivations that prompt donors to give is so important that I'm going to come back to it later (see point 84, in Chapter Seven).

But don't forget that the best research of all is free. You get it by regularly meeting with and talking to your donors.

TO PROVE THE POINT: HOW THE RNLI DISCOVERED WHY ITS DONORS GIVE

Britain is a seafaring nation with a long and proud nautical tradition. The United Kingdom's third biggest nonprofit, the Royal National Lifeboat Institution (RNLI), has as its mission saving the lives of those in peril on the sea. With over 200 coastal stations dotted around the country, it boasts the largest private fleet in the world, specially designed and constructed lifeboats manned by volunteer lifeboatmen, male and female, who launch their tiny craft into stormy waters at any time of the day or night, to provide a round-the-coast, round-the-clock emergency rescue service that is the envy of the world. For years this august, 180-year-old institution firmly believed that this mission was the main if not sole reason why such a high proportion of the British people hold this cause so close to their hearts and give it such large sums with such regular reliability. This must be, they assumed, because of the nearly 2,000 lives that the RNLI saves, year after year.

But it isn't so, as the RNLI has quite recently learned to its great profit. The real reason why donors support the RNLI in droves is fundamentally different. But the RNLI learned about this only a few years ago and only because it took the bold step of investing in research. It had been around for more than 150 years before anyone got around to asking its supporters this basic question: "Why do you support us?" During those years the RNLI probably had quite the wrong idea about why its supporters give.

This research among RNLI's supporters showed quite convincingly that although no one objects to it, saving lives at sea is not what inspires donors to give to this famous organization. Not at all. Windsurfers swept accidentally out to sea? Serves them right. Rich yacht owners who get into trouble in high seas? Who cares? Drunken Soviet sailors who fall overboard in a Force 9 gale? Throw them back!

What the research showed so convincingly was that donors give to RNLI not because they feel sympathy or concern for those many souls who get in trouble on the high seas. No, they give because they are thrilled, inspired, and in awe of the heroism, courage, and self-sacrifice of the volunteer lifeboat crews who at risk of their lives launch themselves into untold dangers to save people they don't even know.

That's why the RNLI donors give. It's a very powerful motivation, much different from concern about saving lives at sea. Donors love heroes. Ask Greenpeace, Médecins sans Frontières (Doctors Without Borders), Amnesty International, the cancer nurses, the international development agencies, and a host of others.

Do you imagine that this realization made any great difference to how RNLI goes about its business of raising funds? You bet. The difference is crucial. This simple understanding transformed RNLI's fundraising beyond measure.

18
Recognize fundraising's
three most important words.

Surprisingly, these three words are not "I love you." They're not even "Here's my money" or "We need more." No, this three-word phrase is something much more instructive and challenging but, ultimately, much more helpful too.

If you can keep your head when all around are losing theirs . . . it's just possible you haven't fully appreciated the situation.

Recently a postgraduate student named Paul McFadden, at St. Mary's University, Minnesota, undertook some research into major donors' attitudes to leaving a charitable bequest, or legacy. He identified significant longtime donors who had already decided to leave one or more bequests and sent them a detailed questionnaire. Among the many interesting insights this research uncovered, one was quite stunning, and on its own clearly makes the most powerful case for getting good at this thing called stewardship, or relationship fundraising.

Paul asked his respondents if they had notified the nonprofits of their choice that a legacy was coming. Most had not, and the reason they gave was consistent. It seemed they didn't want to inform the nonprofit that a legacy was coming while the chance remained that they might change their mind and revise their will, leaving the nonprofit out after all. One particular respondent put this so forcefully that Paul followed him up. But he had to access this donor through a financial adviser. In response to the question, "Why haven't you notified the nonprofit of your intention to leave them a major bequest?" the donor had simply written: "May change mind."

The reason Paul was particularly interested in this specific donor was that he had indicated his intention to leave the bulk of his wealth to just one nonprofit organization—an organization entirely in the dark about what might be coming its way. And he'd also answered the question about how much he was intending to leave. The sum was confirmed to Paul by the financial adviser. It was $100,000,000.

To any fundraiser from a North American nonprofit who is reading this, I have a further four simple, important words of counsel: It could be *you!*

Rather a lot, it seems, is riding on that one donor's potential to change his mind. And he's far, far from being alone. As voluntary giving is just that—entirely voluntary—this donor's position is, I believe, not the exception; it's the rule.

The case for brilliant stewardship, I think, is made. It's summed up in those three, devastating little words. All of our donors, at any time, "may change mind."

19
Plagiarize creatively.

I enthusiastically urge you to perfect the art of creative plagiarism. Why should you labor to reinvent the wheel? Why struggle to think of your own big idea if you can borrow someone else's? Plagiarism is the most sincere form of flattery, and we should encourage it at every opportunity. As an author I long ago realized that plagiarism is inevitable and so learned to lie back and enjoy it.

The satiric songwriter Tom Lehrer wrote an engaging lyric about plagiarism:

> *Plagiarize,*
> *Let no one else's work evade your eyes,*
> *Remember why the good Lord made your eyes,*
> *So don't shade your eyes,*
> *But plagiarize, plagiarize, plagiarize . . .*
> *Only be sure always to call it, please,* research.

Few situations for fundraisers are completely new. Almost invariably someone has been there before you and you can learn from them. And what's more, fundraisers are lucky, for they belong to a profession where plagiarism isn't frowned upon; it's even encouraged. We don't have to always call it research, for we work in one of the most open, sharing, and supportive of competitive professions, one that's generally quite honest too. So it makes sense for you to benefit all you can from the experiences, mistakes, and breakthroughs of others. Success is all that your employer is interested in, not where it comes from. But it is good manners to always acknowledge your sources, and as you can rarely get away with just straight copying, it's often necessary (and good practice) to add touches and embellishments of your own. Those who stand tallest are almost invariably standing on the shoulders of those who went before.

The agreeable anecdote in the accompanying To Prove the Point story shows the impact of the new and the advantage of being early, even first. But mostly it shows the value of learning from others, of creative plagiarism. It also illustrates perfectly my next two points.

TO PROVE THE POINT: ETHIOPIA'S FIRST ENCOUNTER WITH FUNDRAISING DIRECT MAIL

Among the most unlikely of places on earth to find brilliant fundraising would surely be the beautiful but trouble-torn East African country of Ethiopia, home of many of the world's poorest people. But fundraising in Africa is developing fast, and a few years ago a young woman of Italian descent named Nadia Weber, working for the Ethiopian branch of the nonprofit Canadian Physicians for Aid and Relief (CPAR) and its Plant a Tree program, found herself in a training workshop run by Bernard Ross, perhaps the best and almost certainly the most entertaining fundraising trainer in the world. It was a lucky meeting for both as it gave Nadia an idea for innovative fundraising and gave Bernard what I think is undoubtedly one of the fundraising world's best case histories.

That day Bernard's agenda came to a premature close. In a spare half hour at the end of the day he decided to introduce his diverse audience to some of the basic principles of direct-mail fundraising, more as general background than in the belief it would have practical application.

Young Nadia didn't say much, but she had that rare ability to learn quickly from others. In particular she took careful note of the samples of direct-mail packages that

Bernard showed. She thought if these can work in other countries, why not in Ethiopia, where the need is so great and where, despite the poverty, there were some people who could help her cause (which was to fight the rampant deforestation currently ravaging Ethiopia's countryside).

Nadia took her notes and some sample packages back to her home in Addis Ababa, and with a little long-distance help from Bernard she put together what was certainly Ethiopia's first ever direct-mail fundraising appeal. It was also an appeal package that any fundraising guru anywhere in the world would have been proud to have created.

All the ingredients were there—letter, leaflet, reply form, reply envelope; competent, colorful, complete. The letter is a model of brilliant, emotive writing. I'll reproduce just the opening paragraphs here. (The letter is printed on both sides of the paper; one side has the letter in Amharic, one of the most common languages in Ethiopia, and the other is in English, as for many in Ethiopia English is the language of business.)

> Dear Friend,
>
> One of our greatest pleasures when we were kids was joining our fathers for forest fruit collection and hunting. Together we would flounder in the thick forests listening to the call of the beautiful music of the forest creatures.
>
> We are ashamed to admit it, but today we can't introduce our grandchildren to the same pleasures. In many places the trees and forests of our countryside have been completely cleared, not withstanding one generation's greed, and therefore denying future gen-

erations of their basic needs. Needs such as clean air, drinkable water, productive land, clothing and shelter.

Fortunately, there are people in our community who have recognized the dangers. . . .

Brilliant, evocative copy. I so envy the way she used the word *flounder*. It paints a perfect picture.

So she had her letter, but who was there in that not very well off land to send it to? There are no commercial list brokers in Ethiopia, and few if any lists to rent. Then Nadia showed how enterprising a fundraiser can be. She took the Addis Ababa telephone directory (a slim volume) and arranged for the letter to be mailed to 500 addresses from it as a test. Her reasoning was that if you owned a telephone in Addis, you were a prospect.

Then she (and her trustees) waited with bated breath for replies to come in. She arranged for a volunteer to collect the replies. Responses had come in, but not as many as she'd hoped.

The trouble was that in his half-hour lightning tour of direct-mail fundraising, Bernard Ross had neglected to tell her what levels of response to expect. That first mailing brought in a response of 40 percent. But Nadia was devastated. What had happened to the other 60 percent? Why hadn't they responded?

Those of us who habitually struggle to achieve just 1 percent in acquisition mailings can only gape in awe.

The mailing attracted much attention, as it deserved. A group of the trustees duly approached Nadia. "We are important trustees," they said, "yet we are not mentioned in your interesting letter nor does the letter give detailed statistics on our project impacts and outcomes." So when it was time to send the letter again, it was accompanied by a four-page densely packed leaflet, a message from the important men on the board (one that even their mothers wouldn't wish to read). Rather predictably response fell, quite steeply.

20
Don't just adopt, adapt.

Merely adopting someone else's experience and applying it directly to your situation is indeed unlikely to work all that well.

The quickest way to double your money . . . is to fold it in half and put it back in your pocket.

Creative plagiarism involves putting in a little bit of yourself. You have to add your own magic touches and ingredients to maximize the original idea's effectiveness in your environment. You have to adapt the idea to your market, your donors, your situation, your specific circumstances.

21
Never believe "that won't work here."

As Nadia's effort showed, it will. Even though you might have to make some allowances for different cultures and traditions, what works in one country or market will almost inevitably work anywhere.

But at international workshops and conferences on fundraising the cry inevitably goes up that the latest great idea or effective technique "won't work here." Fundraisers need to see things more positively. In fundraising a little faith goes a long way.

22
Make the 90-degree shift.

Fundraisers often seduce themselves into the trap of thinking about their work in terms of techniques and methods—direct marketing, major gifts, telemarketing, face-to-face, bequest marketing, special events, and so on—rather than thinking about their different groups of donors and how to build relationships with them.

The 90-degree shift is a vital part of being donor-led. An easy enough approach to describe and to write down, it is perhaps one of the most difficult to practice naturally. But all the techniques in the world will amount to little without it, and perhaps short of winning the jackpot in the lottery, almost nothing will make your fundraising more successful than learning to automatically implement this

Sometimes it is better to beg forgiveness . . . than to ask permission.

simple attitude of mind. Attitude, technique, approach . . . none of these words are sufficient to describe it. Observing when to make the 90-degree shift should be a way of life.

The 90-degree shift is nothing more complex than seeing things from your donor's point of view rather than from (or in addition to) your own or your organization's point of view. It is putting yourself in your donor's shoes, seeing your communication and even your role as a fundraiser through your donor's eyes rather than through the eyes of your CEO or your head of finance or fundraising. Some may say it is really a 180-degree shift, but that is a moot point.

Sounds simple enough, even trivial (though uncomfortable, perhaps). But once you start to practice the 90-degree shift, nothing will ever be the same again.

Consider the following two job descriptions (which come from the book *The One-to-One Future,* by Don Peppers and Martha Rogers (Piatkus, 1994):

> *The brand manager's task:*
> To persuade you and 26.7 million other faceless consumers to buy all the boxes of Frosted Flakes that Kellogg hopes to sell this quarter.

> *The customer service manager's task:*
> To figure out how to increase Kellogg's share of perhaps 1,800 or more boxes of dry cereal that you will buy in your lifetime.

The objective in both will amount to the same thing. But the first is expressed from the company's viewpoint and the second from the customer's viewpoint. Fundraisers need to be customer service managers, not brand managers.

Here are three old and wise marketing sayings to further illustrate the concept:

When a customer buys a quarter-inch drill, what he really wants is a quarter-inch hole.

It doesn't matter what you want to sell. The only thing that matters is what they want to buy.

People don't read advertisements. They read what interests them. Sometimes that includes an advertisement.

The idea of the 90-degree shift is a basic concept, but I believe learning to implement it as second nature is the most important single thing you can do as a fundraiser.

You can find examples of the 90-degree shift in almost every aspect of daily life. I recommend the search, as looking for these examples hones the fundraiser's listening and perception skills. A while back I challenged my wife, Marie, saying I could find the 90-degree shift in almost anything. She responded with a healthy "prove it," and suggested I locate an instance from the radio play we were then listening to (we don't get out much), which was *Three Act Tragedy* by Agatha Christie.

As requested, I searched and quickly found this passage, from the lines of leading actor turned sleuth Sir Charles Cartwright: "The police are searching for clues to prove the butler guilty. So we shall look for clues that prove him innocent. That's not at all the same thing, you know."

A perfect example, I think you'll agree, of the 90-degree shift. (It turned out that the butler's disappearance was a red herring, and instead of fleeing the scene, he had been otherwise disposed of. The guilty party was in fact . . . but I think you'll have to read the play. I recommend it; particularly if you don't get out much either.)

TO PROVE THE POINT:
ROBBIE BURNS HAD
THE RIGHT IDEA

Robert Burns, Scotland's national poet (and therefore mine too), is for many the greatest of all romantics. So his work should appeal to fundraisers everywhere (show me a fundraiser who isn't at heart a romantic).

To my mind the most important thing Burns ever said, for fundraisers or anyone else, comes in a few lines

from one of his lesser-known poems, "Tae a Louse." The
lines I'm thinking of go as follows:

> *O wad some Power the giftie gie us*
> *To see oursels as ithers see us!*
> *It wad frae mony a blunder free us,*
> *An' foolish notion:*
> *What airs in dress an' gait wad lea'e us,*
> *An' ev'n devotion.*

For the non-Scots among you, this means: "O would some
Power the gift give us / To see ourselves as others see us! /
It would from many a blunder free us, / And foolish notion: /
What airs in dress and gait would leave us, / And even
devotion."

Every so often we need to see ourselves as others
see us, truly and clearly, not just in terms of our appearance
and behavior as we ask the public for money but in our
demeanor and presentation at all other times too. This
applies particularly when we communicate with our publics,
whether by post, electronically, by telephone, or face to face.

I have to say it worries me that so many fundraisers
seem unwilling or unable to put themselves in their donors'
shoes, to follow the lessons of Robbie Burns's apparently
simple advice. We will have to get better at this, or the
prospects for our industry, I suspect, are dire.

To emphasize this point, consider if you will the final
verse of "Tae a Mouse," Burns's somewhat complementary
poem to "Tae a Louse," in which the poet addresses some
words of comfort to a poor creature whose home, with the

best of intentions, he has accidentally destroyed. For his
own benefit as much as the mouse's, he observes:

Still, thou art blest, compar'd wi' me!
The present only toucheth thee:
But Och! I backward cast my e'e,
On prospects drear!
An' forward, tho' I canna see,
I guess an' fear!

23
Aim to be fifteen minutes ahead.

Not withstanding cowboys and Indians and cops and robbers,
today's fundraisers have almost without exception been raised
on a near-constant diet of stories
about invaders from outer space:
Doctor Who, Star Trek, Star Wars,
Alien (1 through 5), *ET, War of the*
Worlds, Space Monsters Abducted
My Mother, and so on. These timeless tales of extraterrestrials invariably revolve around the notion of
space creatures arriving from galax-
ies light years from ours to conquer

Only two things are
truly infinite—the
universe, and
human stupidity . . .
and we can't really
be too sure about
the universe.

our puny planet and its pathetic inhabitants, the earthlings,
us. They are, equally invariably, creatures who are technically
vastly advanced when compared with us—light-years ahead,
with craft, weapons, and minds immeasurably superior to ours.
It's generally assumed that overrunning our civilization will

be a piece of cake for invading aliens, because they are so far advanced and we're, well, I suppose, kind of feebleminded by comparison. Our fate is not helped, of course, by the fact that we earthlings are still fighting among ourselves—something aliens wouldn't dream of doing.

But like all caricatures, this reflects only one view. The great American comedian Woody Allen had a somewhat different vision of how our species would be eventually overtaken and subsumed by creatures from outer space. He foresaw swarms of invading aliens who would not be eons ahead of us at all. Instead they would be just fifteen minutes ahead. But they would be fifteen minutes ahead in *everything*. Their eventual victory over our species would be no less certain because of this. In fact it might well be more so.

By being consistently just fifteen minutes ahead, or so Woody Allen believed, these infuriating aliens could always be sure to have just enough of an advantage over us to beat us soundly. They'd always head the line at the supermarket checkout, always be first to grab the last available dryer at the Laundromat; they'd be first to predict the winner of the World Series or the Super Bowl or to spot who would be first across the line in the Grand National at Aintree. In fact, whatever plan, scheme, or ruse we pathetic earthlings might deploy to save our species, these infuriating aliens would inevitably be there just ahead of us, constantly beating us by a nose, always enough in advance to unfailingly gain the upper hand because of their unerring ability to be just fifteen minutes ahead.

What on earth, you may be thinking, has this got to do with donor development?

At first glance the desire to be fifteen minutes ahead may seem something of an alien concept to fundraisers, but I find it stunningly practical. Being just a bit ahead underpins most of the fundraising successes enjoyed by fundraisers I've worked with over the years—and I'm sure features in most successful fundraising case histories around the world. It's all about not wasting your energy trying to catch the distant, elusive BIG IDEA, but instead focusing your creativity and skills on catching all the little ideas that are swimming within easy reach around your feet.

The point is, these days it's really, really difficult for fundraisers to find the new big idea, to come across the one big thing that will set them light-years ahead of all their competitors. Many try long and hard to find their big idea. Few succeed and most are sadly disillusioned. And it gets harder and harder for those who have come along most recently.

But there are still literally hundreds, perhaps thousands, of ways that fundraisers can be fifteen minutes ahead of their competitors. There are still innumerable ways that could easily get you just that important little bit in front of the rest. And in these demanding, competitive times, each of these may be just enough to give you all the edge you need. Taken together, they will for sure propel you and your organization well ahead of the crowd and into a quite different league, ensuring all the success you could possibly wish for.

I hope you'll find quite a few ways to get fifteen minutes ahead within the pages of this book. They are there for sure, but you may have to look for them. Success is like that, I find. It comes to those who look for it and avoids those who don't. Some of the ways to be fifteen minutes ahead that this book presents may leap out of the page at you; others, I guess, will require a little interpreting and understanding from you, maybe even some light digging.

But they are there for sure. And I'm certain that if you look you'll find some of your own too.

24
Keep well informed and up to date;
never imagine you know it all or are even close.

Keeping informed takes work, but it's worth it. British fundraisers in particular seem content to wallow in professional ignorance. We buy far fewer fundraising books than our American, Canadian, or Australian cousins, and I suspect we're generally less well read (and so less well informed) than most of our European counterparts too.

Whatever your nationality, read the latest books and articles (see my recommendations in points 77 and 78, in Chapter Seven) and go to the best seminars with an open mind, not just to network but to learn. Because most of your competitors won't do this (they're either too lazy, insufficiently involved, or too arrogant to realize they don't know it all), this is one easy way to get and stay fifteen minutes ahead. Knowledge, I have learned, comes not to those who see, but to those who see well.

Take a notebook with you to these seminars and write down (neatly, so they can be deciphered later) all the good ideas you'll have if you keep your mind sufficiently open. Look around you at all of your fellow delegates who have neglected to do so, sitting there, arms folded, and with glazed expressions. They might look less self-satisfied if they knew that they just fell fifteen minutes behind, but the probability is that they will never realize it. Don't be like them.

It's a grave mistake to believe you know it all—and to fail to realize that your seminar presenter can easily tell how little you are actually taking in. For the presenter, you might as well have the word *dork* tattooed on your forehead. Nevertheless, from the presenter's viewpoint, the minority who do make good use of seminar time more than compensate for the others' shortcomings. I just wish they were a higher percentage. Or perhaps it's just me and my seminars . . .

I conduct a lot of seminars, around the world, and it saddens me to so often see whole rows of delegates who clearly think they know it all. It's easy to tell because these people write nothing down. We presenters well realize that if as many as a handful among the forty or fifty in our class actually do anything different after listening to us then we've done well indeed. Most will do no more than jot down a few of our pearls, nod in agreement with our more obvious generalizations, and then quickly forget about them, although perhaps absorbing some of our wisdom or pithy anecdotes as if by osmosis. But even that's tolerable compared to the substantial group who appear to assume it beneath them to even take a note. It may be an exaggeration to say that speakers at seminars merely fill in the boring bits when the bar isn't open, but fundraisers, to their cost, too often think they already know all that's worth knowing.

Quite why they are there is another matter. I think it's a question that should be asked.

TO PROVE THE POINT: "HUH—I ALREADY KNEW THAT!"

People often remark on how lucky I am because I get to present fundraising seminars in exotic locations around the world. I usually agree, when I reply, but go on to point out that the harder I work, the luckier I get. Not everyone appreciates the irony.

Some years ago I found myself at a fundraising conference in the UK, attending a session called "Frontiers of Direct Mail," or something similar, a panel discussion featuring many of Britain's most successful fundraising direct marketers. Sitting next to me in the audience was a young account manager from a marketing agency of my acquaintance, just a few weeks

If you lend someone $20.00 and never see them again . . . it was probably worth it.

into the job. After the presentations she couldn't wait to deliver her verdict.

"Huh," she exclaimed with contempt, "that was nothing new. I already knew all that."

"Well," I replied, trying to be sagelike, "I know what you mean, but funnily enough I took six pages of notes nevertheless."

She delivered me a withering look, which showed that her scorn for me knew no bounds. She didn't have to say so, for I could sense her smugness as she flounced off thinking, "Fancy that, I know more than Ken Burnett."

25
Learn the lessons of history and experience.

Perhaps not surprisingly, modern fundraisers think they started it all, so it's all right for them to imagine they know it all too. But this is a mistake.

Fundraising is perhaps the second oldest profession. It's mentioned in the Bible. Most of Europe's splendid cathedrals, built in the Middle Ages, were paid for by a form of fundraising (often accompanied by the promise of boiling in oil if your donation was in any way deficient).

It would be shortsighted and foolish indeed if we were to overlook the lessons we could learn from those who have gone before, but we'll have to change our approach because, if recent history is anything to go by, ignoring these lessons is surely what most of us do.

 ## TO PROVE THE POINT: BRILLIANT FUNDRAISING FROM THE DAYS OF JACK THE RIPPER

Fundraising will progress only if we can be creative and innovative in new product development (see point 13, in Chapter One). But we'll be effective at that only if we understand and appreciate all the innovation and development that has gone before. We don't need to reinvent the wheel, just to improve it and keep ensuring it still goes round.

A while back I was rummaging among the archives of a great British charity, The National Society for the Prevention of Cruelty to Children (NSPCC) (see point 69, in Chapter Five), when I came upon an appeal letter personally written by the founder of Barnardo's, another great British institution dating back to the poverty and squalor of Victorian London. For more than a century this august organization, originally called Dr. Barnardo's Homes for Waifs and Strays, has been a pillar of British child-care provision.

Further digging by a friend at Barnardo's unearthed
several brilliant letters to donors written by the founder,
Dr. Thomas Barnardo, at the turn of the nineteenth century.
One particularly impressive epistle, dated 1888 (the year
when Jack the Ripper began his bloody rampage through
London's East End), ran to four pages and featured short
sentences and paragraphs, lots of underlining, bold highlights, indenting, multiple postscripts, a headline, and a
direct proposition, not to mention a great case history. It
even started with "Dear Friend." In short this relic of a by-
gone age employed virtually all
the techniques, devices, and ingredients that we now habitually

**Never put off until
tomorrow . . . what
you can avoid
altogether.**

use in our direct mail and believed
we had recently invented. Other
stuff they used in days of yore
included offering incentives (1886),
source code tracking (1934), member-get-member schemes,
and lots more besides. Technically these early examples of
our art were in no way inferior to what we produce today.
Often they were much better (introduce twelve friends in
1886, and Dr. Barnardo would personally send you a solid
silver brooch or tiepin, plus no doubt another four-page
personal letter).

The thing is that up until I stumbled upon this
insight a dozen or more years ago, I seriously believed we
had started it all, that it was me and my generation that had
given birth to the basics of modern fundraising communication. And so it seemed did every other fundraiser I showed
these early materials to. In all probability we had labored to

reinvent the wheel, because in our arrogance we failed to look at and learn from the experiences of our predecessors.

To underline the last ten points, here are *five cautions:*

- *Expect inconsistency.* Common sense is rare. Don't expect people to apply common sense regularly or consistently— or even at all.
- *Constantly reiterate.* Everything has been said before, but because so few people really listen, it has to be said again and again. Most of the time fundraisers don't read, don't listen, and don't learn. Many donors are like that too (though as they are volunteers they can be forgiven).
- *Learn to read people accurately.* Donors will often tell you what they think you want to hear (because they're nice people). So because what people say to us isn't always the whole truth, we have to learn to *really* read people.
- *Delve deeper.* What people say they'll do is often quite different from what they will do in practice. Beware of this, and dig a bit deeper to discover the real meaning of your research findings.
- *Never assume.* It would pay us all to have these two words, if not tattooed on our foreheads, at least displayed in large letters above our desks. When in doubt, check it out.

Chapter Three

KEEP REVISITING THE BASICS

19 Gold Nuggets: The Solid Foundations of Fundraising

F or the introductory chapters of my book *Relationship Fundraising* (Jossey-Bass, 2002), I prepared a list of the many wise sayings that I've picked up in my long years of fundraising. Many of these have been around for generations, most are common sense, some may appear hackneyed or overly sentimental, but all are important advice for would-be fundraisers. A version of the following nineteen points should be given to every new fundraiser as he or she takes the first steps in his or her career. And ways should be found to place this list regularly before more seasoned practitioners too. We'll all be much more effective fundraisers if from time to time we remind ourselves of the foundations. (I've edited this list slightly, to avoid duplication of points that appear elsewhere in this text and expanded the descriptions where appropriate to fit better with the format of this book.)

26
People give to people.

I hesitated to include this point, because it's so widely known and well worn among fundraisers as to be almost a parody. But

Give a man a fish and you will feed him for a day. Teach him to fish . . . and he will sit in a boat and drink beer all day.

we'd be fools not to regularly revisit even the most basic of the basics, because they're what most people overlook in practice. So, take note of this piece of the blindingly obvious: people give to people, not to plans, projects, organizations, mission statements, or strategies. Fundraising is all about one person giving something of what they have to help another in need. At its heart it is one individual giving to another.

27
Fundraising is not about money.

At least not primarily. It's about necessary work that urgently needs doing. Money is the means to an end. It talks, sure. But it can't sing and dance. If as a fundraiser you start by asking for money you won't get it—and you won't deserve it.

28
Be a donor yourself.

This is seen by some fundraisers as a controversial and even scandalous suggestion, but I think it is essential. How can you inspire a donor to give if you don't give yourself? "But . . . ," I hear some fundraisers say, "I already work so hard for these people. That's how I give."

Phooey!

What a load of hogwash. If your belief in your cause isn't strong enough to elicit a small part of your own disposable income, it won't be strong enough to sway many donors.

Besides, you learn such a lot as a donor. So you should give to other causes too, to see how they care for and nurture their donors, and pinch all their good ideas.

But of course giving is voluntary, so as an employer I wouldn't compel you. You decide.

29
Friend-make before you fundraise.

At its most simple, effective fundraising is about being nice to people. There's not enough in it to fill a page, far less a book. Yet this most basic of all the basics is the one most often overlooked. Fundraising isn't a negotiation; it's a compact between friends. The arm we once believed we should twist up the donor's back, we now realize should be draped around our shoulders in friendship.

People give to people they like—and trust and care about. So it will help you if your donors can view you as a friend—and vice versa.

But be careful how you do this, and in particular always make it clear to potential donors that you are a fundraiser, so there will be no surprises when, later, you ask for money. Just as you should never sell to friends or family, at least not without their explicit, willing compliance, you should guard against allowing your loved ones to have any feelings of obligation to give just because it's you asking.

30
Fundraising is about needs.

One of the first axioms I learned as a fundraiser is that people applaud achievement but they give to meet a need. There is some truth in this saying. Fundraising is about meeting needs and not celebrating achievements. Though I've learned over the years that as donors come to know more about the needs of your organization they will be reassured by and even come to depend upon the organization's regular achievements if they are to keep

The Romans did not create a great empire by having meetings . . . they did it by killing all those who opposed them.

giving. And when you are celebrating achievement can be a very good time to ask for money to meet a new need.

But donors must clearly see and understand your non-profit's needs, or more precisely, the needs of the people it exists to help. On its own, what the nonprofit is achieving is insufficient reason for donors to keep on giving. So you have to keep finding creative ways to remind donors of the need.

31
Harness the simple power of emotion.

It takes real skill to master and wisely deploy the simple power of emotion. And this ability is one that many fundraisers struggle with and some fail at utterly, often because they fear emotion or, at best, misunderstand it. Sensitive exploitation of emotion's full potential is integral to effective fundraising. It's a tool fundraisers simply must learn to use.

Of course fundraisers can never neglect the paramount need to be legal, decent, honest, and truthful, and so must guard against misuse and inappropriate exploitation of emotion. But we fundraisers shouldn't hang back from the opportunity that the power of emotion provides to open people's hearts and minds. Reinforce your requests with facts, statistics, and logical arguments and never forget that emotion is a drug that should be used with care. But also be well aware that nothing will draw your donors in and bind them to you like raw emotion.

32
Offer a clear, direct proposition.

My favorite headline is this direct offer:

Make a Blind Man See
$20.00

Where else in the world could you get such value for money? What an incredible thing to be able to do. A British nonprofit ran a version of this headline on its press advertisements for years. Thousands gladly responded.

The beauty of this ad is in the direct, relevant, easily imaginable offer. So give your donors a direct proposition, something they can relate to. If you can put an easily affordable price on it, so much the better:

Sponsor a dog and make a tail wag, $12.00 each month.
Introduce a child to the magic world of books, $5.00.
Save a mile of California coastline, $973,600,000.

You get the idea.

TO PROVE THE POINT: CLOSE ENCOUNTER WITH A HAIRY YOUTH

Recently I was visiting an agency I work with in Reading, England. I had just left the railway station when I was stopped in my tracks by a shaggy-haired young man with a bolt through his bottom lip. Very politely, given his menacing appearance, he asked me for 70 pence so he could buy a second-class train ticket to Banbury, a nearby town.

I was puzzled at the specific nature of the sum requested (I gave him £1.00, as it happens), so I asked him about it.

"Why 70p," I asked, "is that all a train ticket to Banbury costs?"

"No," he replied, clearly shaken by my ignorance, "it's £2.40. But I asked you for 70p because you looked like you could afford that."

I was very upset. Not even a pound! I reeled at this slight, mentally regretting my casual decision to leave off a necktie that day. Sensing my dismay my new young friend said reassuringly, "Usually I just ask people for 50p and think I'm lucky to get it." I was so relieved I nearly gave him another pound there and then . . . but I didn't want to spoil him.

He went happily on his way (though I doubt it was to Banbury). And I was left pondering the advantages of knowing how much to ask for from each prospect and the importance of presenting the request as a direct proposition.

Of course, if that shaggy-haired young man had really known what he was about, he would have taken my name and address so he could have solicited me later for a monthly gift . . .

33
Open hearts and minds first, then wallets.

This is a sequence worth remembering each time you prepare to clinch a gift. It will help you avoid a condition to which fundraisers are especially prone, sweaty palm syndrome. This affliction frequently comes on just before *the ask* (this new noun, I fear, is here to stay in our profession). Sweaty palm syndrome occurs when the fundraiser hasn't sufficiently prepared the ground by finding appropriate ways to add the inspiration that makes asking all but redundant. Usually it's inspiration and information cleverly presented that will open hearts and minds.

So don't just ask—*inspire*. The fundraiser's role is much more than just asking for money. That's perhaps the least and almost the last of all the things we do. Merely asking is in no way sufficient. We have to inspire people to give. Fundraising is the inspiration business.

34
You don't get if you don't ask.

Very often that's true. At some time or another fundraisers must overcome their fears and actually ask for the gift. It's one of the oldest clichés in fundraising: if you don't ask, you won't get. But perhaps we should add to it the word *properly*.

Because success in fundraising is not about what we do but about how we do it. You won't get if you don't ask *properly*.

In many instances, of course, fundraisers don't wish to do the asking themselves but must identify, recruit, train, and equip others, usually volunteers, to do their asking for them.

Asking is a very special skill, so it pays to select the right people for the job. Good askers are often good listeners and will have a great deal of sensitivity and affinity for others.

Teamwork means . . . never having to take all the blame yourself.

Intuition and the ability to read people really help too. Good timing is also crucial: When is it the right time to ask? When is it best to wait? Persuasive, possessed of good communication skills, well organized, likeable, committed, of the right peer group . . . it's not easy to find good askers, and often they're in great demand (so nurture them well and reward them appropriately if you want to keep those you have).

But most important of all is willingness and even enthusiasm to do the asking. Of course any experienced asker knows that there are few more rewarding feelings than the one that comes when, after a challenging presentation, a donor finally confirms a major gift. The buzz gained from securing a major gift for a worthwhile cause can be considerable.

35
Share problems and successes.

There's a lot of sharing in fundraising. Ideally fundraisers and donors should share the same point of view about a non-profit's cause, and it'll help if they share other interests and passions too.

But it's a mistake to focus on sharing only the good things. Donors invariably respond well to the full story and in the right circumstances will be your organization's staunchest allies when things go wrong. A full explanation and a positive spin will help too, but don't hold back from sharing problems. Donors will find successes more credible when problems are aired too.

36
Identify and present your organization's distinctiveness, its *brand*.

The best definition I know of the term *brand* for a nonprofit is, "the set of ideas, images, feelings, beliefs, and values that are carried around in a person's head." It's the beliefs and values that distinguish nonprofit brands from commercial brands—though beware! Many corporations are now stealing our clothes, posturing as socially responsible enterprises, and laying emphasis on their beliefs and values too. We don't have the monopoly on good intentions (just as they don't monopolize sharp practice).

Though some may tell you different, a strong brand identity isn't everything for a nonprofit, but it really can help. A strong brand isn't just how the organization looks. Think of brand as personality. Donors need to be able to easily differentiate between causes, and if your organization stands out clearly from all others, it will be recognized and remembered, and will prosper as a result.

A brand is much more than just a smart logo. A logo is mostly about presentation and outward appearance. You don't judge a person by his snazzy suit and tie. What are your organization's characteristics, what gives it individuality, what's

69

different and distinctive about it? What are its beliefs and values? Never forget that it is the nonprofits with strong, clear brands that attract the most legacies, or bequests.

37
Be great at storytelling.

However sophisticated we become, at the heart of our business quite simply is the ability to tell stories. I know I've said this before and I will again, because it's important. Fundraising is and always will be all about storytelling: human interest stories, engaging stories, touching stories, involving stories, inspirational stories, moving stories—all of them welcome, well judged, well timed, well illustrated, and above all well told: concise (if possible), believable, and memorable. Do this job properly, with flair and passion, and the rest of the advice in this book will all fall neatly, easily into place, and donations from your keen supporters will flow in, sufficient to meet your organization's every need.

Eagles may soar . . . but weasels don't get sucked into jet engines.

Fundraisers must be storytellers *par excellence*, the best in the business. It's a skill that over years is trained into actors and authors, con artists and charlatans, priests and street vendors, but that's been neglected for far, far too long by the fundraising profession. This won't do.

For we have some of the best stories in the world and the best reasons of all for telling them. Fundraisers deal daily with real drama; life-or-death situations are our constant fare. Human interest abounds in what we do. We can tell tales of courage and self-sacrifice; of neglect, nobility, despair, humanity and inhumanity, suffering, hope, and enlightenment; of triumph over seemingly insurmountable odds. From preserving the planet to restoring the school roof, from breakthroughs in medical research to saving the whale, we're rich in the raw materials of storytelling. More than most businesses we have at our command an abundance of words and pictures that combined together will far exceed the sum of their parts in their power and passion to convert good intentions into action.

We just have to get better at doing it.

Here's a tip: the story you have to tell best of all is the story of your organization's mission—in other words, why your organization exists and what it does. That's what donors will come back to again and again. The succinct story of your organization's mission will sustain them in supporting your cause through the ups and downs of their lives, and in the end it's the story that will most likely influence (or not) their decision to leave a bequest to your organization. So it's worth making your mission statement the very essence of what your nonprofit is about, a good story well told.

38
Great fundraising is *not* selling; we offer donors a relationship of shared conviction.

There is one fundamental way in which a charitable gift or donation will differ from any commercial transaction. The nature of the relationship between the fundraiser and the donor isn't at all the same as the relationship between the buyer and the seller. Buyers and sellers partake in a relationship of shared commercial interest. Donors and fundraisers enjoy a relationship of shared conviction.

It's a difference well worth remembering, particularly if people are constantly telling you that fundraising is really just a form of selling. The simple truth is that donors don't want to be sold to. They will resist it at every turn. Donors don't want to be telemarketed to or to know that fundraisers train in the use of enticing body language or seductive face-to-face techniques. While we strive to perfect all of our multiple methods of communication we mustn't identify ourselves with methodologies designed merely to part our donors from their money. We'll succeed far more if, rather than viewing us as high-pressure salespeople, donors see us as sitting on their side of the table, partners and not adversaries, friends who genuinely have their best interests at heart. That's not selling. Good fundraising is more about sharing than selling.

That said, the effective fundraiser needs all the skills of a professional salesperson and a few more besides.

39
You can turn complaints into support.

Your organization's most loyal donor, researchers have found, is the donor who has complained and been responded to appropriately. If you think about it, this makes sense. Complaining donors are people who care. If you can resolve the cause of their complaints, they'll love you for it and will even go around telling their friends. This is a fantastic piece of information. Instead of keeping our heads down and hoping donors will be really gentle with us, maybe we should be encouraging them to deluge us with complaints . . .

Or maybe not. But for sure we should be giving donors the opportunity to complain and not be discouraging them or making it difficult for them, as most nonprofits do.

For the reverse of this finding about complaints is certainly true too. We know, because research has told us, that a dissatisfied customer who doesn't complain to us (so we can assuage his concerns and woo him until he loves us even more than before) will go out and tell at least a dozen friends and acquaintances what a disreputable, ineffective, and generally crappy outfit we are. And we don't want that, so we should go to great lengths to avoid it.

Because they're generally really nice people, most donors don't like to complain to a nonprofit. Often they'll make extreme allowances for the nonprofit before they'll think or say anything critical, but mostly if they're dissatisfied they'll keep discreetly and usually unhappily silent. So we won't know what the problem is, and therefore we can't put it right, which means more unhappy donors in the future. Not a satisfactory state of affairs.

We shouldn't hide behind this tendency of donors to be very patient and forgiving of nonprofits. We should really encourage donors to complain and make it as easy as possible for them to do so. Set up a telephone help line. Put names and faces on your organization's customer service staff and proudly publicize their phone number to all and sundry. Explain the level of service the organization aims to provide and why it matters that people tell the organization quickly if ever it falls short.

Put another way, we need to reassure our donors that their satisfaction (and confidence and trust) really matters to us.

There are obvious costs associated with this. But obvious benefits too. However don't ask your donors if you should do this or not. They don't wish to be a bother and will urge you to save the money. You'll have to judge for yourself what the right level of service is and then invest, or not, as you think best. (See also points 59 to 65, in Chapter Five, on customer service.)

40
As donors grow older the importance of trust and confidence in the nonprofits they support increases.

Trust and confidence in the nonprofits they support are both vastly important to donors. Both imply some expectation of how an organization will behave, but trust differs from confidence in that it is implicit and doesn't rely on direct experience or any practical knowledge of the organization. Trust can be assumed, whereas confidence usually is earned and based on some personal or reported experience.

The beatings will continue . . . until morale improves.

Both trust and confidence appear to grow in importance as donors get older. Fundraisers should understand and cultivate trust and confidence, for they could be the difference between receiving a bequest and missing out. Donors who support seven to ten causes in their lifetime, on average leave bequests to only two or three. So we fundraisers should construct all our strategies around the objective of building easier, stronger, and more automatic ways for donors to comfortably and unreservedly place their trust and confidence in our organizations.

I think my colleagues in the development nonprofit ActionAid International have expressed the commercial reasons for this very nicely in their *Fundraising Strategy 2006–*

2010: "Although banks have been allowing us to manage our relationships with them online for many years most charities are a long way from this. The future will not be Supporter Relationship Management, but rather Supporter Managed Relationships. Virtual communities are becoming more and more important to people. Virtual marketing is an opportunity that is only going to get bigger. It will be the charities that can let go and become facilitators of their supporters' relationships, rather than the controllers of them, that will succeed in the long term."

I'll go along with that.

41
Avoid waste.

Donors really hate waste. Wasteful behavior from a nonprofit implies that a donor's gift too will be wasted, which in the backs of their minds is what donors fear most when they give a gift. So we fundraisers should go out of our way to show that our organizations are not wasteful and that in fact the reverse is true—they are adept at making a little go a very long way.

Among the many elaborate and expensive color brochures that I've seen fundraisers send to donors as part of welcome or thank-you packs, one of the simplest and most effective came from the development department of a PBS TV station in the American Midwest. It was a simple color postcard—itself a joy to receive—hand signed by each of the five folks in that department, all sending their appreciation and best wishes to the lucky donor. It cost pennies, but spoke volumes.

All our agencies, designers, and communications advisers love to persuade us toward smart, colorful, and expensive design and presentation, but almost invariably (as long as the content is reasonable, relevant, and interesting), what looks cheap and cheerful will produce the best response. Most supporters will respond most positively to the amateurish-but-enthusiastic look, one that clearly shows money isn't being wasted on expensive materials. Makes sense, doesn't it?

42
Technique mustn't obscure sincerity.

Donors will be wary of technique and may not like it. The professional fundraiser, it seems, is still not widely admired or understood in many quarters. Donors certainly want to see competence in the nonprofits they support, but they are often suspicious of professionalism. If they were to know how fundraisers routinely profile, target, segment, and set out to seduce them, they might well not like it, to say the least.

Fundraisers of course rely on a range of skills and techniques to do their jobs and are always seeking to advance and improve their methods. But more than people in most commercial areas, fundraisers need to be careful to keep technique in its place. You may be delighted to hit a 0.01 percent increase in response to your latest acquisition mailing, but that figure wouldn't impress a donor. So fundraisers thrive when they can constantly emphasize the beliefs and values and the commitment, passion, and sincerity that all underpin their singular approach to their jobs.

Donors want to see your sincerity come shining through in everything you write, say, or do. Of course, as the great British actor Laurence Olivier was fond of remarking, once you can fake sincerity, anything is possible. The sad truth, however, is that most fundraisers just can't fake sincerity at all convincingly.

Yet from the fundraising that comes through my mailbox, down my telephone, and even face-to-face, it seems to me that professional fundraisers attempt to fake sincerity regularly, often on a daily basis. But they rarely succeed at it. As Olivier would also have confessed, faking sincerity is about the hardest of things in his profession. For fundraisers, I think it isn't really worth the effort of trying, as donors will almost always spot your artifice.

When everyone else is being told to "think outside the box" . . . that's when you should start to think *inside* the box.

The *Oxford English Dictionary* defines *sincerity* (and I paraphrase a bit here) as the state of being honest, frank, genuine, free from pretence or deceit, clean, pure, believable. I think this definition worth posting prominently on a wall in every fundraising office. We should all aspire to get these qualities into all our fundraising.

TO PROVE THE POINT: SOME WAYS WHERE FUNDRAISERS ARE GOING WRONG

Fundraisers are ferocious bandwagon-jumpers. A few years ago my agency Burnett Associates conceived and wrote a truly brilliant direct-mail pack for our client Amnesty International. It was Amnesty's banker (that is, best-performing appeal package) around the world for years. It told the gruesome story of a young man who was tortured by having his eyes put out with an ordinary ballpoint pen. The mailing enclosed a small plastic pen and said, "what you hold in

your hand can be an instrument of torture or it can change
the world."

"Go on," the powerful copy says of the small
plastic pen that was attached. "Tear it off the page. Hold
it in your hand. Feel the point. Think about it. . . . Stretch
your imagination. Because that's what torturers around
the world do. They excel at it: using their imaginations to
fashion instruments of torture out of the most everyday
things."

Great copy—"use the pen we've given you as an
instrument of change, to change the world." The thing is
that in attaching a free pen to this pack, there was a rather
obvious point. It worked well, as you can imagine.

Then suddenly everyone was doing pen packs, even
when there was no logical reason to include the free pen.
Fundraisers turned the addition of a free pen into a cheap,
offensive, off-putting gimmick.

The advent of questionnaires, or survey packs,
with which pen packs are often combined, followed a similar pattern. At first, Greenpeace included a questionnaire in
a direct-mail package because it genuinely wanted to know
its supporters' views on a range of issues. It turned out that
the questionnaire stimulated response as well. In time this
approach too became a bandwagon. Soon everyone was
sending prospective donors questionnaires, mostly with no
intention of evaluating, or even of looking at, the responses
so thoughtfully and painstakingly completed. They still
abound, these survey packs, though most donors saw
through them long ago and learned to treat them with the
contempt they deserve.

Closer Encounters

We fundraisers are often not much better when we meet donors face to face. Here I distinguish between the American use of the term *face-to-face fundraising,* which usually describes peer-to-peer solicitation, and the European use, which describes stopping passersby and signing them up to monthly electronic debits. Initially, at least, people in most countries tolerate face to face (street) fundraising, and some find it involving. But there's a limit to how many causes the average passerby can support with a monthly gift. And if you are accosted on a daily basis by these tabard-clad fundraisers as you go to work and again as you come home, the initial attraction quickly palls and turns to dislike, even contempt. Most people find this kind of face-to-face fundraising irritating and intrusive. People don't like to constantly have to say no, particularly to a worthy cause.

The modern day equivalent of, "Buddy, can you spare a dime?" is the deathly banal, "Can you spare a couple of minutes for Alzheimer's?" or some similar request. The people who do this surely highly dispiriting, draining job have come to be seen not as inspirers but as *chuggers* (an unflattering descriptor, shorthand for *charity muggers*).

A bit extreme, perhaps (muggers hurt people and steal from them). But the truth is that more and more people every day routinely cross the street to avoid fundraisers. As a result of the public's growing distaste it surely won't be long before this highly successful recruitment method will be restricted legally. Regrettably but understandably, public aversion to the way nonprofits practice this form of fundraising means this particular golden goose will soon be for the chop.

THE ZEN OF FUNDRAISING

Bad for fundraisers and also, I suggest, for the public's perception of the causes fundraisers represent. How many bequests have been deleted from donors' wills, following one unwelcome encounter too many with these chuggers? We'll never know. But logic suggests it will be quite a few.

The Future of Fundraising Is . . . Gold Foil!

At a seminar I attended in the United States recently, a range of direct-mail packs was displayed from the podium, and the audience members were invited to guess which treatment worked best in terms of response.

All the mailings on show that day featured the same formats, design styles, creative treatments, and ways of presenting their cause. All were excessively dull. The only thing that differed from pack to pack was the type of tiny, trivial incentive included (not perhaps surprising as the session was sponsored by a mailing company that specifically promotes premiums). These incentives, we were solemnly informed from the podium, are the only really important ingredient when it comes to influencing response. They included Easter seals; personalized name and address labels; Christmas seals, cards, gift tags, and paper; holiday name labels; prayer cards; seed paper; badges; color die-cuts . . . and of course patriot seals (featuring the Stars and Stripes). Oh, and changing the reply envelope's color can help too. As can an outer envelope copy line such as, "Your beautiful holiday labels are enclosed."

The cause, it would appear, makes very little difference. What matters in direct-mail fundraising, we were told, is the choice, style, color, and prominence of the premium or incentive. Just one of the many informative lines that issued from the podium was, "We're not here for the long term. We can't wait." Hardly an appropriate sentiment for fundraisers, particularly as we so depend upon bequests.

Do not walk behind me, for I may not lead. . . . Do not walk ahead of me, for I may not follow. . . . Do not walk beside me either. . . . In fact . . . just leave me alone.

But the moment of truth came when we in the audience were asked which we thought would win in a test between patriot seals and gold foil labels. We waited, breathless, . . . the gold foil won, hands down!

At this a frisson of anticipation raced round the room. Simultaneously it dawned on each of us: What if you could test putting gold foil actually on the patriot seals?

Answers on a postcard, please, to the publisher. There's no prize.

43
Write it down, stick it on the walls, circulate it to trustees.

Once you have captured the essence of your distinctive approach to fundraising don't file it away in a drawer or a dull report. Create a definition and a list. Highlight all the pithy phrases and the punchy summaries. Stick your list on your wall where all can see it. Make sure all your fundraisers and all staff who meet the public have a copy. Send it to your trustees—and maybe some of your donors too (point 69 shows how one organization does this).

44
Fundraisers are talented people, so make sure they're always shown due respect.

My list of the fundamental foundations of fundraising could easily go on and on. They show just how rich and diverse fundraising is but also how demanding. If fundraisers are to succeed they clearly need to be multitalented and highly competent as well as creative and inventive. It should go without saying that fundraisers have to be resourceful, optimistic, consistent, courageous, determined, gregarious, adaptable, personable, and have a quirky sense of humor. There may well be hundreds of other adjectives that would be at least as appropriate. Being a fundraiser is a challenging and multifaceted job—and far from easy. Fundraising demands people with very special qualities and abilities, and it offers them endless opportunity and variety.

Never test the depth of the water . . . with both feet.

Important components of fundraising success include being appropriate, getting results, innovating, using your imagination, using new technology creatively, displaying patience, and of course, being modest and unassuming!

The points set out in this chapter are universal, but my text here is almost certainly not comprehensive and may exclude some important principles and procedures that relate particularly to your organization. Have fun adding your own ideas and concepts to my far-from-complete eighty-nine.

Chapter Four

GETTING YOUR MESSAGES SPOT ON: APPRECIATED, UNDERSTOOD, AND REMEMBERED

14 Keys to Communications That Reach In and Grab Audiences

I t may just be that the most important question for most fundraisers is, "Do your supporters really read what you send them?" The answer of course is mostly no. This could be very depressing for fundraisers. But it's also another opportunity to get fifteen minutes ahead.

I've often wondered why fundraisers produce such a huge body of dull literature when the raw materials of which they write hold so much dramatic possibility. For as long as I've been a fundraiser I've been attracted by our profession's potential for fine writing and simultaneously dismayed by how little fundraisers make of it. You just have to look at the missives from nonprofits that stack your own mailbox. *Inspirational* isn't the adjective most people would use to describe what we routinely send out. *Dull* would probably be selected ahead of *delightful*. *Wearisome* would most likely take precedence over *welcome*. If we really believe we do such urgent, necessary work, it seems to me a crying shame that we don't convey our messages better, particularly in words. What we do is so striking, so urgently needed, and so full of what a scriptwriter would consider great storylines. Yet it seems beyond us to describe what we do in terms that will have our prospective readers simply begging for more.

I'm sure this is very much a matter of using words better. For on their own, pretty pictures convey only a part of any story. True, words too need to work well with their accompanying illustrations. But it is the careful, cunning weaving together of words and images that becomes compelling, invigorating communication of the kind we fundraisers should routinely wing our donors' way, to remind them constantly of the great things they make possible when they support our cause.

45
Why communications matter.

Researchers have at last got round to proving what most of us have known instinctively for years—how we communicate with our donors is of the very first importance. Studies in the UK by the prestigious Henley Management College have concluded that when it comes to building trust and confidence with donors, the quality of ongoing communications is the most important component. I don't find that even a tiny bit surprising. Our communications are the window through which we invite donors to see our nonprofit's work and the purpose of that work, its achievements, its personality, and how it has performed as a steward of their generosity and good intentions.

No, it's not surprising that communication skills are perhaps the most important qualifications of a fundraiser. That's why I gave the subject such emphasis in my list of key strategies in Chapter Three. What is surprising is how bad at communication most fundraisers and fundraising organizations are.

46
The changing media
and audience environment.

People . . . they're curious and really rather marvelous, in their way. As individuals they may be a bit of a mystery. But put them together and with actuarial precision you can be sure that particular people will behave in certain predictable, particular ways. Whatever their country, color, race, religion, or ethnic background, on so many levels people are the same everywhere. They don't change. The things that move them, inspire them, anger and excite them, motivate and depress them, turn them on and turn them off, all tend to be consistent across similar groups of people, whatever language they speak or culture they come from.

Come what may, people will always be people.

That's true for sure. But there are important ways in which people do change. When times change, behavior, fashions, interests, and preferences all change, sometimes rapidly and fundamentally. As a result, what was acceptable once or what worked once may not be acceptable or may not work now. People nowadays seem to be changing more rapidly than at most other times in history, particularly in terms of what they are willingly prepared to take time and trouble to read and understand. For "our" readers (whom, by the way, we share with dozens, perhaps hundreds, of what others may perceive as equally if not more compelling and worthy causes) the commodity of time seems in ever-diminishing supply and their attention spans appear to shorten by the month. So many messages now clamor for our donors' attention in an average day (each person is exposed to at least 800 different promotional messages every day, maybe lots more), and these are so brash, colorful, well written, and well illustrated and produced with such big budgets behind them, that it's now really difficult for anyone producing free communications to penetrate the ambient din that pervades our readers' lives.

For the producer of unsolicited communications from a nonprofit, this is important stuff to know. As is how to cut through the noise and clutter to secure our rightful share of mind with each and every one of our donors.

In fact this may be the biggest challenge that fundraisers face.

47
Be firmly reader-led.

If your communication stands any chance of being read, far less remembered, then it has to be delivered in a form people will find inviting, with images that will catch their eye and content they will really want to read. For your message to get through, people need to be open, receptive, and willing to be persuaded to pay attention. So anyone who produces free-distribution publications just has to be guided morning noon and night by the concept of the 90-degree shift. Your publication will be noticed, read, and remembered only if it presents what they, your readers, are willing, even eager to read, rather than what you and your organization might want to say.

Communicating with donors isn't any more difficult than that.

48
Talk to donors where they are, not where you want them to be.

We also have to talk to donors where they are in terms of their interest and understanding, and not where we might hope or even assume they are (although if you take the final caution in Chapter Two to heart, you'll never assume anything).

If we wish to be understood, we must talk to people in ways they will understand. Despite the apparent simplicity of this point, it's an area where we easily make mistakes. For example, fundraisers are often young, socially aware, liberal, somewhat left-of-center people. Many donors are older, tending to be conservative, more inclined to caution, and perhaps leaning a bit to the political right. This shouldn't mean fundraisers and donors can't find common ground on which to communicate (after all, both care passionately about the same cause), but it does mean we fundraisers have to realize the difference and adapt our approach to suit our audience.

This point is particularly crucial for campaigning organizations. Often fundraisers assume that a nonprofit's donors have a greater knowledge of or level of interest in the nonprofit's cause than they actually do. So the fundraisers infuse their communications with jargon, talk in acronyms, or refer to complex issues and background that the fundraiser might understand and be interested in but that mean little to the average donor. If you want to avoid incomprehension and blank looks, talk to people where they are, in language they can understand. You'll soon find it pays.

Just to make life difficult, however, the opposite of this is just as much of a problem. We mustn't patronize or oversimplify.

Fundraisers have to pitch it just right—not easy, but challenging.

49
Offer involvement at every opportunity.

We need to transform our communications from their present one-way focus into a genuine dialogue. We have to invite our readers' participation. So, on the inside front page of your brochure, magazine, or annual report, list your organization's key people and their contact numbers. Put in photographs to make them seem more real and approachable. Encourage contact enthusiastically. At the end of each article or individual story, invite your readers to contact you or a specified individual in your organization, so you can know their views. Offer further information if appropriate (e-mail is often the cheapest and easiest way to do this). List other relevant sources. Let readers know their input is welcome and important to your organization and that their further involvement is encouraged. Even if most readers don't take you up, don't be discouraged by the limited reactions you'll get at first. It builds, and if most people seem to prefer to be passive, it doesn't mean they're all not interested. But do realize that some are and do all you can to attract and involve them.

No one is
reading . . .
until you make
a mistake.

Finally, always put a donation request and fundraising contact details somewhere on everything you produce; remember, though, that sometimes it's appropriate to make this quite discreet. It does no harm to reinforce constantly your organization's continuing need for funds. Real donors expect it. But don't always shout your need for funds at them.

50
Offer a good conversation . . .

The communications sent out by most nonprofits are gray, drab, uninviting affairs. Inevitably, it seems, they're dull. Yet if we were telling a friend about what we do, we wouldn't dream of being less than scintillating or anything other than compelling. If we met someone at a party who asked us what we do, we'd be riveting. So why are we dull in print?

Apart from deciding not to scare or perhaps bore people with too many words, it's also good to decide to avoid pompous *organization-speak*. All corporate language and jargon should be eschewed in favor of an easy, conversational style. Read your copy out loud. If it sounds hard to digest or might risk boredom and disinterest in a casual listener, work at it again to inject more human interest. Your communication will be more enjoyable and involving if it speaks to people as if you were in conversation with them, talking—one human being to another—in everyday language designed to transmit enthusiasm from you to your listener or reader.

Let the passion come through. In their rush to professionalize, many organizations lose their fervor and dissipate their sense of purpose. This is another chance for you to get fifteen minutes ahead.

51
. . . not a good speech.

Fine words alone don't make for good fundraising copy. It's how you use them that counts. Remember the old Roman aphorism, "When Caius spoke in the Senate the people said, 'That was a remarkably fine speech,' but when Marcellus spoke they shouted, 'Let us now march on Byzantium!'" For Marcellus's powerfully put words had moved his listeners not to sympathy but to action. Nice though it might be, we don't want our donors to applaud our fine communications. We want them to be moved to do something.

TO PROVE THE POINT:
IN PRAISE OF THE POWER
OF FINE WORDS

Recently, on the chance recommendation of a friend, I consulted the views of that gloomily prophetic British novelist George Orwell (he of *1984* and *Animal Farm* fame), which I found in his 1946 essay *Why I Write*. Orwell was, apparently, an awkward old cuss, but he sure knew how to use words well.

George Orwell claimed four great motives for writing prose:

- Sheer egoism. Desire to seem clever, to be talked about, to be remembered . . .
- Aesthetic enthusiasm. . . . Pleasure in the impact of one sound on another, in the firmness of good prose or the rhythm of a good story. . . .

- Historical impulse. Desire to see things as they are, to find out true facts and store them up for the use of posterity.
- Political purpose. Using the word "political" in the widest possible sense. Desire to push the world in a certain direction, to alter other peoples' idea of the kind of society that they should strive after.

Well, good on you, George. Couldn't have put it better myself. Fundraisers, think of these four when you come to plan your next direct-mail pack.

Orwell went on to say, "When I sit down to write a book, I do not say to myself, 'I am going to produce a work of art.' I write it because there is some lie that I want to expose, some fact to which I want to draw attention and my initial concern is to get a hearing. But I could not do the work of writing a book, or even a long magazine article, if it were not also an aesthetic experience."

Fundraisers too often approach the production of a direct-mail appeal, a fundraising brochure, or even a book about fundraising as if they were trying to produce a work of art rather than trying to get a distinctive message across. They start confined by the formats and formulas of their craft, rather like an artist beginning with concerns of how his or her picture will be framed, hung, and lit rather than with the thoughts, emotions, or solutions he or she wishes to convey. North American fundraising communications, particularly, all look and sound desperately, dismally alike. This is because they are tied to formats and formulas laid down as if by inviolable decree by direct marketing and communications agencies, to make their lives simpler.

In his essay *Why I Write,* Orwell continued as follows:

> All writers are vain, selfish, and lazy. Writing . . . is a horrible, exhausting struggle, like a long bout of some painful illness. One would never undertake such a thing if one were not driven on by some demon whom one can neither resist nor understand . . . it is also true that one can write nothing readable unless one constantly struggles to efface one's own personality. . . . Looking back through my work, I see that it is invariably where I lacked a political purpose that I wrote lifeless books and was betrayed into purple passages, sentences without meaning, decorative adjectives and humbug generally.

Here Orwell is exposing the tendency other writers have to take the lazy way out, perhaps because they're insufficiently involved. For fundraisers this should never be good enough. Fundraisers have to believe that they must change the world.

Writing for the purpose of fundraising shouldn't ever be easy. It should be a struggle driven by at least two irresistible demons, overwhelming urgency and utter conviction, unshakeable belief in the rightness of the cause.

Encouragingly, it seems to me that there is a realization slowly dawning among fundraising professionals that effective communication really is the core of our craft. The more farsighted among us are now aware that fine pictures and fancy design are not enough. It is the effective combination of words and pictures, chosen so that together their sum far exceeds their parts and skillfully woven into stories that will hold our donors spellbound and inspired.

As if to drive this point home, my friend, former colleague, and the second George in my tale, George Smith, has just produced a little book designed to help fundraisers use words more wisely. It's called *Tiny Essentials of Writing for Fundraising* (White Lion Press, 2003). At one point in it he offers the following observation: "I suggest your heart would soar if—once in a while—you received a letter written in decent English which said unexpected things in elegant ways, which moved you and stirred your emotions, which angered you or made you proud, a letter which you wanted to read from beginning to end, a letter apparently written by one individual to another individual. For you never see these letters any more."

Isn't that amazing? Doesn't it make your heart soar just to imagine receiving such a thing? And doesn't it then sink when you realize the travesty that most of our fundraising letters have become?

Oh my, such is the power of words. Pictures show, but words shape the imagination. George Smith resolutely believes that for nonprofits better writing is a direct route to raising more money. He rails against "the age of bullshit" and the modern propensities for spin, prolixity, and predictability. He is cantankerous about sloppy writing and relentless about the necessity to get your thinking right and the need to steer clear of the many stultifying, dehumanizing processes that surround writing for fundraising.

If ever a profession needed to appreciate the power and potential of fine words, it is fundraising.

52
Say less but better.

Fundraisers frequently fail to get their messages across because they try to say too much. When you are asked to approve copy, one good rule is to request that the writer cut it in half. Extend this practice to the number of publications your department produces. Are they all needed? Do they all justify their cost? Couldn't most of them say what they need to say more concisely, and wouldn't understanding improve if they did?

A person who smiles in the face of adversity . . . probably has a scapegoat.

This self-analysis might lead to some savings in what you print and produce. The wise fundraiser will reinvest the money thus released into improving the content of the communications that remain.

53
Remember, a fundraising organization is a truck.

Your organization's function is to deliver loads of benefits from donors (your readers) to beneficiaries. The organization shouldn't come between the readers and their understanding of what their gifts achieve. So it should never occupy center stage (think how many nonprofits you know that do). As it effortlessly conveys and connects donors to the cause, it should ideally remain discreetly in the background. Donors don't really want to know about the organization. They want to know what it and its fundraisers are doing to advance the cause.

Your communications can be a bit like a truck too, in that their function is to convey to donors loads of words, pictures, and images that have been structured to inform, entertain, and inspire to action.

54
Be regular.

Regular, planned communications keep donors in touch, informed, and involved. If you are irregular in your communications, be aware that other fundraisers are not so lax. They also have access to your donors, so they'll be in touch when you are not.

55
Design for readability.

Choice of typestyle (roman, italic, and so forth), typeface (font), column widths, measures, and leading, and use of color, tints, and backgrounds—these may all seem unlikely fare for fundraisers, but they're vitally important considerations if you want to communicate effectively with your nonprofit's donors. Fundraisers are prolific publishers, so it's not surprising that some basic technical understanding is necessary for all of us who really wish to reach our readers. A glance at a selection of magazines, leaflets, newsletters, and annual reports produced by nonprofit organizations will show how sadly deficient fundraisers still are in this regard.

Of course we all now invest more in color printing and fancy design, but few really understand the business of communicating in words and pictures enough to avoid the many pitfalls and make it easy for readers to access and enjoy what's on their pages. Desktop publishing and other technological advances haven't really helped fundraisers much. Our tendency to do things on the cheap when we don't have the skills to do them well has often set fundraising communication back rather than propelled it forward.

These days electronic communication is every bit as important as the printed page. Here it pays to be brief and appropriate and to always offer the donor relevant choices.

In printed communication a most common mistake is inappropriate use of type, particularly the choice of a sanserif rather than a serif type for body copy (if you don't know the difference between these families of typefaces, that rather proves my point).

If the task of producing your nonprofit's communications is not in the hands of someone who really knows how to communicate using words and pictures, I suggest you transfer it to someone who does. You wouldn't leave your wife's eye surgery or your children's education to someone who only vaguely understands what he or she is doing, would you? This should be no different.

 ## TO PROVE THE POINT: A TEXT TO INFLUENCE ALL COMMUNICATION EVERYWHERE

An interesting book appeared a few years back on the use of type and related subjects. Called *Type and Layout: How Typography and Design Can Get Your Message Across—or Get in the Way* (Worsley Press, 2005), it was written by Colin Wheildon, an academic researcher in Australia. Wheildon's book soon won cult status among many experienced communicators, but it was almost entirely ignored by members of the graphic design industry on both sides of the Atlantic.

The dramatic findings in Wheildon's book are all based on painstaking research with groups of typical readers over many years in many formats, using lots of subjects in several countries. Apart from choice of typestyle and typeface, Wheildon also studied layouts, reading gravity, justification, type size, letter spacing, colors, tints, backgrounds, and other aspects of communication in relation to readability. Use and abuse of these factors had not previously been quantified, and their impact on readability was frequently ignored by designers.

Sadly for the design business, Colin Wheildon found conclusively that would-be communicators pay a massive price whenever they depart from the perhaps conservative standard of a serif type of a reasonable size, leading, and line width, printed in black on a white paper background. Staggeringly important though this finding is, designers find it inconvenient, limiting, and boring, so most choose to ignore it. In fact Wheildon confirmed many assumptions that have characterized good communications for years, but because the graphic design and print industry finds his conclusions inconvenient, his work has been shunned, or at best neglected, and his book was out of print for many years. Now it has been reissued by the Worsley Press and can be ordered on Amazon.com.

Care for Your Readers with Older Eyes

In his book, Wheildon describes the problem with sanserif type, as discovered by researchers of the British Medical Council in 1926. The description is detailed so I won't reproduce it here, but basically people knew back then that to use sanserif type for large amounts of body text was bonkers. The common theme, verified by almost all of Wheildon's tests, was that readers had difficulty in maintaining concentration, owing to the absence of serifs and the type being too regular. Wheildon found this to be particularly true for readers with older eyes (the kind of folk who support many nonprofits).

Designers claim this is nonsense and that in time readers will get used to sanserif type and even come to love it. Wheildon dismisses this as analogous to claiming that by changing your children's breakfast cereal from Wheetie Pops to wood shavings, they'll come to love that too.

If the text is short and of a reasonable size (as in short headlines, call-outs, or standfirsts), Wheildon reckons that very small amounts of sanserif type are OK, because its use doesn't much affect readability. But what does Wheildon say about sanserif type for body copy? In comprehension studies, whereas roughly two-thirds of a newspaper's readership will comprehend a given article set in Garamond (serif), that comprehension level will drop to one-eighth when the same text is set in Helvetica (sanserif).

Oops! This isn't a teensy, inconsequential difference we're talking about here. We're actually looking at comprehension being five times less, simply because of a change of typeface. With that kind of risk there have to be very compelling reasons for setting body text in sanserif type. "It's the brand style" certainly wouldn't qualify, unless your brand values include being almost unintelligible to just about everyone.

See It in Your Daily News

Could this explain why almost no major newspapers choose sanserif faces for body copy? Many magazines, however, do. They also frequently set their type in colors other than black on white, reverse their type in great chunks (sometimes out of tint panels and even out of halftones), run type round pictures and across pictures, and commit other obvious abominations. Not to be left out, advertisers in these rags regularly commit similar atrocities, showing nakedly in public their designers' lack of understanding of how to communicate through the printed word. People pay to buy magazines. Who cares whether they actually read them? (Apart, perhaps, from the poor souls who pay to advertise in them.)

If communication is the key to building donors' trust and confidence, then it really is essential that we don't make things unnecessarily difficult for donors. So our materials, cornerstones of our donor relationship development strategies, should all be welcoming and easy to read. Fundraisers probably lose up to half the potential readers of their printed materials simply because they squeeze in too many words and set the type too small. They probably lose most of the other half because, unknowingly, they set their important messages in the wrong kind of type or to the wrong measure or on the wrong kind or color of background. Or because they make some other error or omission that would be really easy to rectify if they only employed people with the right kind and level of skills for the important tasks fundraisers do.

At first this may appear to be an additional cost. It isn't. In fundraising communications the real waste is in the vast quantities of materials we produce that are simply never read, principally because their important messages have been wrapped up and presented in such a way that no one of normal disposition would be sufficiently interested, or able, to read them. So don't skimp on this. You can't save souls in an empty church.

56
Build loyalty.

The potential to win or build (or damage or lose) loyalty is obviously crucial for fundraisers. How do fundraisers create loyalty? What might a charity loyalty program look like? Is it about offering rewards, encouraging specific behavior, changing attitudes, or a combination of these methods? If you assume that nonprofits can't have loyalty programs because they can't give discounts or reward points, you'd be wrong. Who says they can't offer discounts? Under the UK government's Gift Aid program, donors can claim a bonus for the nonprofits they support simply by signing a form, which then allows the nonprofit to reclaim the basic rate tax the donor has already paid on his or her gift. What's that, if it isn't a 24 percent discount on a donation?

Always remember, each one of your readers is unique . . . just like everyone else.

Or why not offer points for certain behavior? We can also offer privileges (access, visits, special information, choices).

Loyalty cards or programs don't build loyalty in themselves. They are just a way of saying thank you, of rewarding loyal customers. The secret is that the nonprofit first has to give commitment, excellent value, brilliant service, and communication. And to be loyal itself, to its donors.

Securing donor loyalty could be really good for business. There's an old saying that there are three Rs in loyalty:

- Retention
- Repeat business
- Referrals

This is why you want satisfied, loyal donors—they will stay longer, they'll give again and again, and they'll go out and tell their friends and family to do likewise. Besides, as every fundraiser should be constantly reminded, donors tend to be promiscuous in their giving. So it's really nice if they are particularly loyal to your organization.

The most important factor in developing loyalty is effective communications (just as it is for building trust and confidence). Creating these communications is the skill fundraisers tend to be least versed in but need the most. It's in fostering trust, confidence, and loyalty that good communications really justify the considerable investment they require. Research now shows that when it comes to building trust and confidence, communication is paramount.

TO PROVE THE POINT:
WHY YOU NEED TO DO
LOYALTY PROPERLY

In 1844, when the Rochdale Equitable Pioneers Society was formed in the United Kingdom (in time it evolved into the hugely powerful cooperative movement), the twenty-four weavers who set it up could scarcely have imagined that their dividend would be the forerunner—and with eleven million members the most spectacularly successful—of a flood of customer loyalty programs, from Green Shield stamps and Air Miles to the UK's recent runaway winner, Clubcard, from food retailer Tesco.

Yet there's an apparent contradiction here. Although these days we might call it a loyalty program, the co-op's dividend was really an incentive, a profit-sharing plan for customers designed to encourage them, as the slogan went, to get their oats at the co-op and nowhere else.

Loyalty doesn't seem quite the right word to describe the result of such inducement. It is more like a financial incentive. Take away the incentive—cheaper groceries—and where does the loyalty go then?

Sadly—or perhaps fortuitously—we fundraisers can't buy loyalty, or so it seems at first glance. We're limited in the inducements we can offer because we can't give back anything of apparent financial value that will have any effect on binding the modern consumer to our cause. Maybe, though, we just haven't yet found a successful way of offering it.

But formal loyalty programs don't always work in the commercial world, far from it. The best lesson that's been learned by the few retailers who have succeeded is that their program worked because they did it properly. I wish I had a pound for every nonprofit that has asked, "Will this [some program or strategy] work for me?" My answer is always the same—"Only if you do it properly." Only a few listen.

57
Ensure all communications are seamless.

Don't compartmentalize. Make the 90-degree shift and try to see your cycle of communications as your donors see it: one communication after another, arriving in the mailbox, over the phone, or in the shape of a personal visitor. Do they all look as if they come from the same outfit, or do they appear to have emanated from several different departments that don't talk to each other? Are they all *on brand* (hateful phrase, but you know what I mean)? Do they all consistently reinforce your organization's key messages? Are you sure your organization's donors are enjoying the clear impression you want to make with them? The only way this will work is if you bring all sources of contact together and make them work cohesively.

Fundraisers should stop structuring their departments by function (direct mail, telephone, events, major donors, database, and so forth) and start structuring them around groups of donors.

TO PROVE THE POINT:
HOW DO YOU KILL
A WHALE?

Some years back I was organizing a review of the publishing functions of one of Britain's top charities. It was a huge task because it produced so much: books, brochures, reports, booklets, leaflets, posters, flyers, information sheets, display stands, exhibitions, and so forth and so on. Requests to produce publications came from a vast variety of sources, and the overstretched publications department generally had to do what it was told. This led to some very esoteric publications—my favorite was entitled *How to Kill a Stranded Cetacean.* Although there are unlikely to be many takers for a leaflet that explains what to do if you happen upon a beached whale or an abandoned dolphin, the fact is there's no easy way to kill one if you do find it still alive. And would you want to kill it anyway?

It was all much too much, and my and my colleagues' main job was to rationalize and simplify it all. One of the

What do you do when you see an endangered animal . . . eating an endangered plant?

other excesses we found was the laudable but often impractical aim of producing publications in various languages. So for many publications there would be not only a Welsh language version but also versions in Hindi, Gujarati, and numerous other dialects and languages. Indeed, there may well have been a Gujarati version of *How to Kill a Stranded Cetacean,* although we didn't find it.

58
Putting All Your Communication Needs Together.

Of all the points in this book, this one is perhaps the most important for you to fully understand and act upon. I urge you to read it closely.

Do you, as I do, find yourself frantically searching for updated and approved materials every time you create new publications, or searching for good photos and stories that haven't already been overused? Would you like more time to focus on retaining all those supporters you worked so hard to attract? Do you wish that your magazines, newsletters, or reports were of more interest to more people? Does your non-profit's current infrastructure make it cumbersome to collaborate on case and communications materials with your colleagues in an efficient, effective way? Do you crave a donor communications system so easy to use that it requires no technical expertise, where the software for it can be simply added on top of your existing database? Are valuable fundraising and stewardship lessons lost with every organizational transition?

If you replied yes to any or all of these questions, then you are in the market for one of the new donor stewardship platforms that are, even as I write, being developed specifically to meet the unique communications needs of fundraisers by using and adapting the latest advances in technology and thinking from the world of customer relationship management. Even if you didn't answer yes to these questions, you should still be looking at these developments, for they could be the most significant step forward in the fundraising business in decades.

Imagine if you could access and manipulate all of your organization's and others' best stories and pictures electronically and with ease, from the comfort of your own desktop. If you could develop the best possible communications for each fundraising case and structure them individually for each different type of donor, for each anticipated set of donor interests. If you could allow your donors to choose not just when and how often they wish to hear from you and what they wish to hear about but also the specific issues and subjects that might appear in your nonprofit's newsletter or what most interests them from its annual report. Imagine if you could do all of this and at a readily affordable cost.

You're imagining the future of fundraising communication. It's just around the corner. It has to be, because experience constantly shows that necessity is indeed the mother of invention. And if it is to thrive, modern fundraising has to change rapidly from its current highly unsatisfactory sales paradigm to a new *mind-set* that focuses on relevant and appropriate choice and communication, offering donors genuinely interesting and engaging ways to use their discretionary funds freely and willingly, so that they can enjoy the process of influencing the social changes they want and can take pleasure as they see the differences they make become reality.

We need the technical ability to deliver such a vision. And we need it now. As I see it, there is no other viable way forward for fundraising.

There are many commercial suppliers interested in supplying fundraisers with the communications solutions we now seek. Some of these products will be quite suitable; some will evolve to become suitable; some will be distinctly unsuitable. It will be a complex and congested field and will include many suppliers offering versions of systems for what was once referred to as customer relationship management, or CRM as it is now more commonly known.

My own view is that what fundraisers really need now is a step beyond CRM. Today's CRM systems are not usually designed and run for fundraisers by fundraisers, but they have to be if they are to really deliver what we need from them. What we need is the application of relationship fundraising combined with the latest in database, telecommunications, digital print, and web technology.

Be adventurous, be entrepreneurial by all means, but be careful. Realize that getting this right will just be 10 percent about technology, 30 percent about systems, and a full 60 percent about people.

Whatever you spend on this new area of gear for donor development it's likely to be a significant investment, so it's important that you get it right. Thoroughly check out the field, ask the right questions (this book might help), and go for the system that suits you and your organization best.

Or the prudent course might be to wait until a clear industry favorite emerges. Sometimes it pays to be second, to not be a pioneer. No guts, no glory, it's true, but also no expensive mistakes. But that kind of thinking really doesn't appeal to me. That might leave you fifteen minutes behind, which is not at all what you want.

 ## TO PROVE THE POINT: FUNDRAISING'S HOLY GRAIL MAY BE JUST AROUND THE CORNER

I have no doubt that an easily managed, integrated, comprehensive, donor-focused communications platform will be de rigueur for fundraising organizations in the very near future. For many fundraisers this quantum leap forward is literally just around the corner, and it's about to transform utterly the way we communicate with donors.

If there is a Holy Grail in donor development, in fundraising generally, then it must be the process that seamlessly unites all of an organization's fundraising communications to and from donors. It will be a system that will give all of us easy and equal access to our best resources so we can effortlessly present our most compelling materials in the best, most involving, most motivational, and most effective manner possible in an infinite variety of ways across a bafflingly diverse range of media, on the way easily taking account of and satisfying an expanding range of donor interests and preferences. I believe that the development and arrival of the technology and the "people" systems that will enable us to deliver this seismic change in the relevance and suitability of our communications will be as significant an advance for fundraisers as was the move a few decades back to relational databases. Most fundraisers won't remember these days, when we kept all our donor records in shoe boxes or on Rolodex files, and maintained and accessed manually such information as we kept. But I do. (OK, I know this paragraph has way too many adjectives. But it's a concept that does carry me away.)

It seems a bizarre recollection now, as most fundraisers can't imagine doing their jobs at all without their databases. But the piecemeal and rather haphazard development of the modern fundraising database happened quite recently, within the time that I've been a professional fundraiser. Even then it happened only because we needed it to happen. So it will be with the new communications systems.

Chapter Five

WHAT'S ESSENTIAL?

12 Important Things to Think of When Relating to Your Donors

Sometimes we pay a heavy price for trying to do important and necessary things on the cheap. While we should always avoid waste and false economy, our focus should constantly be not on cost but on value for money.

59
First impressions count:
have a great welcome strategy.

As all actors know, if you fluff your entrance, recovery can be difficult. So develop a comprehensive, effective, "warm and friendly" program to welcome new donors appropriately, to reassure them that the decision behind their initial gift to your organization was a good one. Make your welcome prompt, personal, sincere, and *never* an immediate request for a further gift. Donors may well consent to giving it, but they won't like you for asking for it, and the first impression you will leave with them will not be the one you want. Remember, first impressions last.

60
Operate an effective thank-you
policy and always say thank you properly.

It pays big time to say thank you properly—and promptly. In the apparently mundane process of saying thank you, fundraisers could find the best solution to attrition, the most cost-effective first step toward donor retention (see point 61, later in this chapter).

Thanking donors used to be considered a tedious administrative chore. We know (detailed research now confirms what we all knew instinctively but mostly ignored) that saying thank you properly is one of our best opportunities to get each of our donor relationships off to a great start and to build on it as we go along. Equally, if we get this wrong, it's a chance to screw up everything for good, right from the start.

There are numerous thorough studies of the art of saying thank you for nonprofits. This is not a small thing, to be nodded at in passing. Thanking is a subject that will repay your in-depth study. For this collection of essential things to do, I want to pick out just a few of the really important *keys*.

Checklist for Thanking and Welcoming Nicely

- Survey competitor activity.
- Elevate the thanking and welcoming process in your organization. Make it sincere.
- Thanking is not a finance function. Keep it at the heart of fundraising.
- Thank everyone, whatever the size of the gift. Respond within forty-eight hours.
- Train staff appropriately.

- Always write personally.
- Start a relationship: institute dialogue, ask questions, or offer choices.
- Recruit volunteers to do the thanking.
- Decide on appropriate responses to different types of first gifts.
- Devise a policy for donors who say they don't want to be thanked.
- Prepare a welcome kit or pack for new donors.
- Consider introducing a "welcome back" approach for returning former donors.
- Survey donors' attitudes.
- When appropriate, offer a choice of methods of communication—mail, e-mail, phone call, or visit.
- Set out a donor charter that includes your organization's thank-you policy.
- Offer each donor a breakdown of his or her giving once each year, even if it's zero.

61
Learn three keys to secure
the all-important second gift.

As kids we were all taught to say thank you properly. It was a painful task but a necessity, nonetheless. So whatever gifts we received, wanted or unwanted—Aunt Beryl's inevitable socks at Christmas or Cousin Richard's entirely inappropriate selection of Frank Sinatra hits—all would duly be followed by a communication of appropriate recognition, acknowledging receipt and offering thanks. This was usually in the form of a painstakingly penned letter that followed a rather unimaginative pattern but that was designed to be prompt and to appear both individual and sincere. To offer anything less would have been unthinkable and could be presumed to lead to fewer presents next time round.

Never underestimate the power . . . of very stupid people in large groups.

Fundraisers should learn from this shared past and get smart, following this process more creatively and efficiently than even the most cunning and acquisitive of schoolchildren would ever have dreamed. If you want to secure a second gift—and who doesn't—then, as Penelope Burk of Cygnus Applied Research, Inc., outlines in her book *Donor-Centered Fundraising*, three crucial steps must be followed:

- You have to let donors know you have safely received their gift or gifts. So prompt acknowledgment in the form of a really nice thank-you letter is essential. This should be sent within a few days (no more than two is good) and really shouldn't include any request for a second gift.
- At the same time your donors should also be assured that their gifts will be used for the specific purpose they requested. If the gift is general or unearmarked, tell them the kind of thing you might do with their gift. Make sure it will seem good value.
- Some time between your acknowledgment and thank-you letter and the next ask, you should provide measurable results showing that the donor's gift has been effectively used to carry out his or her wish.

This three-point rule makes sense, doesn't it? It isn't rocket science and is neither very expensive nor difficult to do.

Yet very few fundraisers do it well, despite the incentive that preventing attrition and retaining and involving donors beyond their first knee-jerk gift is probably top priority for most fundraisers.

62
Define and offer *appropriate* donor service.

If you don't do customer service right, your relationships won't even get started. Fundraisers should be very good at it. However, many talk a good talk, but sadly, in practice, most are not good at it at all. The reality is that your donors are more likely to receive quality service and efficient customer care from their bank, insurance agent, or travel company—even their local Burger King—than they are from their favorite nonprofit. If you doubt my word on this, there's a simple test you can try out in the comfort and comparative safety of your own office or home (see the following point, number 63).

For nonprofit organizations the level of service offered has to be *appropriate*, for the cause, the organization, and the donors. Only you can judge what *appropriate* means in your nonprofit's circumstances. To make the right call you'll need to really understand your donors and their relationship to your cause. Plus it'll help if you have a good understanding of what your main competitors are doing in terms of their commitment to customer service. You'll want to be at least fifteen minutes ahead of them (not usually difficult, it has to be said). I suggest you err on the generous side and make your level of customer service just a bit more than your donors might expect. In that way you won't just please your donors, you'll delight them.

63
Road test your own and
your competitors' organizations.

Mystery shopping tests, sometimes referred to as *road tests*, are common commercial practice in many industries in Europe, North America, and elsewhere. Britain's leading consumer's magazine *Which?* does them all the time, as do most other consumer and specialist journals. In a mystery shopping test a fictitious persona is created to put one or more public organizations through its paces, under controlled conditions, to see how good or otherwise it is at responding to a typical customer. The results are always informative and invariably contain some surprises. I have found they consistently confirm the abysmal standards of donor service endemic in the fundraising industry. It's true that almost every time I've mystery tested, one or two nonprofits will emerge as paragons. But these are exceptions that prove the rule that good customer service in nonprofits is patchy at best.

Nonprofits of course hate these tests because they so sharply show up the organization's shortcomings, but I firmly believe in their value and applaud all who use mystery shopping to periodically expose undesirable practices in the dark and hidden recesses of our industry. These tests perform a useful public service, in addition to being particularly valuable for testing your own organization. The most surprising thing about such tests is that most fundraisers seem unable to learn from them (as shown in Chapter One in the To Prove the Point story "The Mystery About Mystery Shopping Tests Is Why We Fundraisers Seem Unable to Learn from Them").

So I recommend you submit your organization, now, to your own mystery donor test. It's not difficult to do. Just arrange for a third party (a reasonably intelligent and properly briefed friend will do nicely) to write, telephone, and visit your organization posing as a genuine donor. You may have to give your mystery donor a small advance of folding money that he or she can use as a gift, but you can console

Once you are over the hill . . . you begin to pick up speed.

yourself that it's going to a good cause. Then monitor closely how he or she is treated (examples of the kind of letter you might write can be found in my 1996 book, *Friends for Life* [White Lion Press, p. 179]). If, as is likely, these tests show up some shortcomings, then change the way your organization treats donors.

If you don't mystery test your organization, believe me, I or someone like me will, sometime soon. And then we'll name names.

64
Implement the service/profit cycle.

There's a cunning device marketers use to illustrate the direct benefits of investment in good customer service. It's called the service/profit cycle, and it is illustrated in the accompanying figure. The encouraging thing about this is that it shows that happy staff are vital for good customer service (makes sense, doesn't it?) and that increased staff rewards are to be desired. So that company Mercedes and the eight-week holiday you've been asking for may not be such an impossible dream after all.

THE SERVICE/PROFIT CYCLE

Customer Loyalty
Retention, repeat business,
and referral

Investment
Spending wisely on service
quality and staff rewards

Customer Satisfaction
Satisfying and delighting
your donors

Employee Satisfaction
Satisfied staff adding value
to products and services

65
Learn twelve keys to
world-class donor service.

- *Be committed.* You and your donor service staff have to really like donors and to be really committed to offering them first-class service.
- *Be properly resourced.* Customer service is something that shouldn't be done on the cheap. The service function needs proper planning and demands the allocation of sufficient resources. If you skimp you'll probably do more harm than good.
- *Be consistent.* Good service raises expectations. People need to know they can depend on certain standards of performance at all times, whenever needed.

- *Be quick.* Delayed responses irritate. Prompt responses please.
- *Be appropriate.* Tailor your response to your donors. Avoid waste and overindulging customers.
- *Be personal.* People like to be remembered and addressed by name.
- *Be recognized.* That way you'll increase your chances of being liked. This is where, as I've said elsewhere, you should publicize your nonprofit's service personnel and show their pictures. Stress they are there only to serve donors.
- *Be meticulous.* Keep first-class records, so you can act on these twelve keys and more.
- *Be there.* You can't go home when your donors need you. If a twenty-four-hour service seems over the top, at least operate a facility for voice messages. It may be that your organization's service department will be in most demand in the evenings from 6.00 P.M. to 9.00 P.M. If so, pay staff a bit extra to cover those hours.
- *Be open and honest.* Never cover up. If your department or organization has screwed up, say so quickly and explain it fully. Donors will love you for it.
- *Be cheerful and helpful.* Never let donors feel that asking is a trouble. That's what you are there for—to help them.
- *Teach customer care to all your colleagues.* I have never forgotten a simple piece of advice from the days when I sold advertising space over the telephone—smile and dial. When you smile while talking on the phone, what you are saying sounds much better at the other end. It really works. Try it. (Tell your colleagues first; otherwise they'll think you've gone mad.)

And if your nonprofit has a voice-mail system, get rid of it by fair means or foul. Seriously. If you think I'm biased, ask your donors if they like doing business with an organization that routes their concerned telephone calls into the black abyss of voice-mail. Then act on what they tell you. (Here I don't mean an automatic answering machine for outside office hours, that's quite OK. I do mean the dehumanized, impersonal, automated voice-mail system that many nonprofits feel is an acceptable substitute for a real human voice to answer donors when they call.)

66
Measure fundraising performance fully.

Most fundraisers measure their performance very crudely, in terms of funds raised now. This may be seriously shortsighted. If you wish to really understand what's going on within your nonprofit's fundraising functions, what's changing and what real value that represents, then you should measure fundraising performance by numerous other important criteria. Commercially, these other measures are often referred to as *key performance indicators*, or KPIs. Perhaps fundraisers would be better served by a series of KDIs, *key donor indicators*.

Some KDIs that might repay monitoring and reporting on in the modern fundraising department are average donation levels, number of donors by type, the ratio of regular (committed) donors to one-time donors, rates of renewal (attrition) among different types of donors, bequest pledges, numbers of former and lapsing donors, number of former donors reactivated, percentages of loyal and superloyal donors (requires definition of these categories), Pareto ratios, number of donor visits, a donor satisfaction index (requires definition and research)—and most of all, calculations of lifetime value. This last KDI is the doyen of them all, the statistical quantification we all want to get very good at measuring so we can see and quantify the results of our stewardship, our assiduous relationship development.

As usual though, this list isn't exhaustive, and you can easily add your own KDIs. All will give you better insight into what's happening within your fundraising strategy than mere funds received will on its own. But avoid paralysis by analysis. Only allocate resources to measuring the genuinely key indicators, the ones that show the differences you are helping to make.

67
Manage well your most expensive assets and resources.

Most fundraisers use a variety of suppliers to help them reach their objectives. Generally outsiders are only brought into an organization to do tasks or provide expertise that the nonprofit itself can't readily, or as efficiently, provide from its own internal resources. This isn't always the case of course, but it should be. Too frequently, fundraisers pay over the odds to external suppliers to do things they could easily and even more effectively do themselves.

Despite the risks and the cost, surprisingly few fundraisers are trained to be good clients. Indeed, few fundraisers aspire to be good clients, and often, if their behavior is any guide, it seems that a substantial number conspire to discharge their massive responsibilities as clients as incompetently as they possibly can.

This is folly of the first degree. In their role as clients many fundraisers will spend more money than at any other time in their lives. That many if not most oversee the process incompetently should be a cause of massive concern to the fundraising community. Perhaps more than any other area, this is where nonprofits could save the most money and most easily improve their effectiveness.

Suppliers are an expensive resource, inevitably. As with staff (an equally if not even more expensive resource), suppliers need clear guidance, thorough preparation, induction, training, and careful deployment. They need guidance and leadership, for you, the client, must always remain firmly in the driver's seat—anything else is an abdication of your responsibility. Suppliers will work better when they are motivated by the cause and the organization they are working for. They'll work better when they are well led and treated fairly. When they are inspired, they'll often go an extra mile or two to supply exceptional value. When they are treated badly, they'll let you down, do shoddy work, or overcharge you, as they would any other dumb nut. Or they'll simply be less able to deliver quality work for you. When I ran an advertising, marketing, and communications agency in London in the 1980s and '90s, it never failed to amaze me how often one or another of our account teams (usually a writer, designer, and account manager) would easily and consistently deliver award-winning work for one of their clients on time and inside budget, whereas they would almost always deliver merely passable work for another, similar client, and then almost invariably late and over budget.

The difference, the only difference, was the client. One was a good client, the other the opposite.

Yet in all the workshops in all the fundraising conferences in all the world that I've ever attended, I've not once
come across a workshop on the subject of how to be a good
client.

Weird, isn't it?

68
Train and encourage your fundraising
staff and pay them well, with more besides.

Most fundraisers work in small shops. Their most frequent
concerns are that they feel isolated and undervalued.

Like most folk who work for nonprofits, fundraisers
themselves are rarely in it for the money (four out of five fundraisers are amateurs, unpaid volunteers). For professional
fundraisers things may have improved in some areas, yet nonprofits still often pay below market rates, and this may be a
spectacularly false economy.

If you treat your staff well, reward them appropriately
(if not necessarily generously), and give them a pleasant environment in which to work, they'll invariably work better and
harder and stay with the organization longer. Treat them
badly, and sooner or later they'll tell your organization's
donors, which will do you no good at all. (This ties in with the
benefits promised by the service/profit cycle.) And give your
staff encouragement and the scope to take risks, innovate, and
explore new territories so they push forward the frontiers of
our profession. Remember Christopher Columbus. He didn't
know where he was going. When he got there he didn't know
where he was. When he got back, he didn't know where he'd
been. But he became famous for it. And he did it on other
people's money.

Happy staff make much better fundraisers. That's just the way it is. So in addition to ensuring all the usual perks for your fundraisers, stress the intangible benefits that go with this unique occupation—satisfaction, well-being, peace of mind, sense of worthwhile achievement. All these add up to fundraising's being a truly great vocation (but staff will still look elsewhere if you don't pay enough).

69
Follow the example of "donor +."

Here's an example of the kind of mantra you might usefully employ to keep your staff aware of and fully engaged with your nonprofit's approach to donors. This internal document comes from one of the UK's leading and most consistently innovative fundraisers, the National Society for the Prevention of Cruelty to Children (NSPCC). The NSPCC prepared this list to encourage and inspire all its staff and to ensure that everyone "sings from the same hymn sheet." But this is no sinecure. It's not a comfortable list to stick on a wall or file away. It really does underpin everything that any NSPCC employee does.

Not one shred of evidence supports the notion . . . that life is serious.

NSPCC'S DONOR +
(Donor + great fundraising = protecting children)

This is our formula for high performance fundraising. It is the way all of us in Appeals can contribute everything we can to ending cruelty to children. These six principles guide us in how we work with donors, volunteers and each other.

NSPCC'S DONOR + *(Continued)*

Passion and Inspiration   The cause of ending cruelty to children is one that inspires people to help change the world. Donors want enthusiastic, passionate staff who clearly care about the cause. We must be inspired ourselves if we are to be passionate about our cause and enable donors to do fantastic things for children.

**Essence: Be passionate, inspired,
and proud of your work for children**

Understanding donors   Dialogue with a supporter—be that face to face or through other routes—should be based on an understanding of the motivation of that individual supporter. We must proactively seek to understand the motivations, values, needs and personality of donors. This will enable us to tailor communications to reflect their motivations and engage with them in what we're trying to do for children.

**Essence: Seek first to understand,
then to be understood**

Open hearts, open minds, then open checkbooks   This is the essential logic of fundraising. We must engage with supporters at an emotional level, then explain to them how the NSPCC is tackling the issue and how their involvement will contribute to that work. For different donors this emotional engagement will take different forms. The emphasis on each part may vary depending on the stage of the relationship but every element is essential throughout a successful relationship.

NSPCC'S DONOR + *(Continued)*

Essence: Engaging hearts and minds
comes before asking for money

People give to help people   Donors give through the NSPCC to help children. They often choose the NSPCC because of its brand and profile but we must always remember that they are giving to children, not the organization. Fundraisers could be compared to a car—our role is to convey donors comfortably to helping children, on the way showing them how and where they can best help. The NSPCC is a donor's agent for changing the world for children.

Essence: We link donors to the
children they want to help

Donors are our partners in ending cruelty to children Our partnerships will be of mutual benefit and often that will mean involving supporters in more than simply giving money. Each partnership should reflect the understanding we have gained of our supporters. We should regularly ask our donors what they want rather than make assumptions. We should enable donors to shape the partnership for the benefit of both children and the donor.

Essence: We must treat
donors as partners in helping children

Donors are for life   *Everything* we do should help build lifelong relationships with our supporters. A donor may be able to help our cause in many different ways at different

---

NSPCC'S DONOR + *(Continued)*

times of his or her life. We need to be flexible and adapt to meet their needs so that we can maximize their involvement. Rather than seeing their gifts as the end in themselves we should see them as milestones on their journey with us to end cruelty to children.

**Essence: Relationships should be
lifelong and develop over time**

70
Benefit from the blessing of inertia.

"Your biggest problem will always be inertia. INERTIA!!! You get up on your soapbox, make your plea, and no one does a thing. That's real life. Most of the people you're trying to move, won't act. But when you use emotions wisely you can overcome some (never all) of that inertia" (Tom Ahern, *Love Thy Reader*, 2005). As he is most of the time, I find, Tom Ahern is 100 percent right here. Inertia can be a real problem, one of the most dispiriting of all the hurdles fundraisers have to overcome. So why would I ask you to benefit from *the blessing of inertia?*

Because, quite simply, as with so many tricks in the devil's hands—fear, mistrust, selfishness, greed, apathy, inertia—it's possible to turn some of his best weapons against him, if we're a bit clever. For all its bad qualities, inertia (and its close ally apathy) is the one that's easiest to get working for rather than against you.

The best example of inertia working in the fundraiser's favor comes with our dear friend the automated bank payment (known in different cultures as electronic funds transfer [EFT], preauthorized checking [PAC], direct debit, or auto-giro). As we fundraisers have clearly proved in recent years, donors are very happy to make regular automated payments to our nonprofits, provided we can give them sound reasons for doing so. Most common are monthly payments, beloved by donors because they comfortably coincide with the frequency of their own salary checks. The beauty of most regular automated payment programs is that to cancel, the donor has to actively issue an appropriate instruction either to the recipient or to his or her bank. As most monthly payments are quite small (or can seem so, despite their tendency to mount up) most donors just don't cancel, even if they want to. They leave the lovely little chaps running. It's too much effort for them to overcome their natural inertia or apathy. Donors appear to think, "Oh well, might as well just let the payments run," perhaps consoling themselves with the thought, "I'll get round to it one day soon." But mostly they never do. Which is good news for fundraisers.

It may be that your sole purpose in life . . . is to serve as a warning to others.

Although it may seem to run contrary to many of the principles I expounded earlier, I have no problem with accepting this money willingly. Were it of importance to the donors, sufficiently so for them to overcome their inertia (which is easy enough if the spirit is willing), then they would do it for sure. For most donors the sums involved aren't of sufficient consequence to bother with. So we can have them!

Chapter Six

WHAT UNDERPINS IT ALL?

6 Vital Characteristics of the Effective Relationship Fundraiser

There are some things in fundraising that should be mandatory, that all fundraisers need to sign up to and practice daily, because if they don't they'll risk undermining public respect for and confidence in fundraisers and in the fundraising profession.

71
Be proud to be a fundraiser.

Our efforts enable good works to happen. Everywhere throughout the world the voluntary sector is growing and increasing its contribution to improve the lot of the human species and to make the world a better place in which to live. Fundraisers play a significant role in this, for without us voluntary action wouldn't happen. We provide the resources that fuel philanthropy. Without our contributions the great machine that is the voluntary or nonprofit sector would grind to an untimely halt.

So we should defend and promote fundraising, but only when we can do so with hand on heart. We should be our own fiercest critics, to ensure that we constantly strive to refine and improve what we do.

72
Believe passionately in your cause.

As a fundraiser you must believe passionately in your cause if you are to have any chance of communicating that passion and commitment to others. Never be ashamed or embarrassed by your passion or afraid to show it in public. On the contrary be proud of it. When backed by the action it inspires, passion such as this is the only thing that has ever changed the world for the better.

73
Be honest, open, truthful.

Shouldn't need saying, this, but it does. Donors expect fundraisers to be consistently and scrupulously honest; they have a right to that. They will repay you harshly if they feel you have let them down. More than on most other professions (except perhaps the police or the clergy), donors expect to be able to rely on what fundraisers tell them. Other members of the public may be less trusting, and this is both a major problem and an opportunity for us.

Generally you don't learn much . . . when your mouth is moving.

74
Be faithful.

Always stick to your promises. Let donors see that you are honorable and trustworthy. Stand by your organization's mission, and don't compromise what it stands for.

75
Be prepared to take a (calculated) risk.

The cautious, heads-down culture of nonprofits these days doesn't engender runaway fundraising success. We seem to think risk is bad and that playing safe is good, that being different is wrong and being the same as everyone else is right. To stand out is to draw attention to yourself. Perhaps people now prefer imitation to innovation. But it's only if we are prepared to take a few carefully weighed and well-calculated risks that we're ever likely to see real breakthroughs.

You're only young once . . . but you can be immature forever.

TO PROVE THE POINT: HOW TO LOOK A GIFT HORSE IN THE MOUTH

Perhaps there is something deficient in our culture. UK management guru Bernard Ross (whom I introduced in Chapter Two) tells an instructive story of a client that illustrates the habitual turning away from risk. The client briefed Bernard to come up with something really new and innovative, a world first. When he duly spread the resulting breakthrough before said client, the client immediately retorted, "OK, Bernard, but what proof have you that it will work? Have you results from anyone else who's tried it?"

My professional career was boosted by a similar incident. I was working for a tiny British international aid charity called ActionAid. It's now one of Britain's top twenty nonprofits by voluntary income, but in those days it was minuscule. A sales rep from a North American specialty printing company came to see me with an invention he believed would transform fundraising as we then knew it (this was indeed some years back, when British fundraising was in relative infancy). I gave him coffee, sat him down, and listened spellbound as he went through his presentation. The product he showed me then was just what I was look-ing for. It was manna from heaven; the breakthrough I had known had to be somewhere, I just hadn't known where. I realized in that instant that his idea would help take my tiny charity into the big leagues.

But I had to ask, "Why hasn't this concept been snapped up long ago by the bigger nonprofits? Why come to me first of all? Why give this opportunity to me and little ActionAid?"

"Easy," he replied. "I didn't offer this opportunity first to you at all. The fact is, you're the only charity who's given me a hearing. No one else has even looked at it."

The promotion I quickly developed from this pre-sentation went on to raise millions of pounds. It also won numerous marketing and communication awards. For the first time in my life I found myself speaking from public plat-forms. A new fundraising format hit the streets, one that has now been used effectively by many nonprofits for many years and is still in use today. ActionAid began to be noticed on the national stage. And me, well . . . I never looked back.

Which is very nice. But what a bunch of dopes the rest must have been! Maybe such a travesty couldn't happen nowadays . . .

Or could it?

76
Be respectful of donors, and show that respect even when they're not present.

The unwelcome but increasingly widespread use among non-profit supporters and even some fundraisers of that unflattering term *chugger* should lead us inevitably to examination of the terms fundraisers often use to describe their donors. Respect from the organizations they support is something most donors automatically expect. But that respect doesn't always follow. Fundraisers, I find, frequently refer to donors and other supporters in terms that might not help their aspirations of building lasting, mutually beneficial relationships.

When we write our fundraising letters we should always imagine we are writing to our mother or someone equally close and vulnerable for whom we'd rather die than offend. And when we gather in our conference halls, seminars, and workshops, we should picture in our minds a group of our donors standing at the back of each room, listening intently to our proceedings. Nothing we say or do should confuse or offend them or make them feel in any way uncomfortable. In the same way as we should respectfully regard our donors we should also picture our beneficiaries, the people our cause exists to help. Such images should not just influence how we behave, what we say, and what we do, they should also inspire us and remind us that when we talk about donors and others we should always show due respect.

This includes showing respect in the labels we stick on donors, the terminologies and titles we use to describe them, singly or in groups. I've always railed against the term *lapsed donors*, for example. It sounds almost biblical, like *fallen women*. How dare they lapse, these people? Worse still are the terms some fundraisers apply to various segments of their databases. I've heard otherwise nice, polite fundraisers refer to groups of their donors and former donors as the *residue*, the *leftovers*, the *dead pool*, and the *sediment*.

How would you like to be thus described? I rest my case.

TO PROVE ALL THE POINTS IN THIS CHAPTER: FUNDRAISING AS A WAY OF LIFE

Perhaps the best British fundraising success story is that of Botton Village, a wonderful oasis of calm and tranquillity set in an isolated, protected valley in the heart of the desolate north Yorkshire moors. Botton seems a typical, rural English village, but there's really very little typical about it.

The village is home to about 350 people, at least half of whom have mental handicaps. The latter live and work side by side in fellowship and community with the other half, who don't have a handicap but who choose to live in this unusual place, in a caring atmosphere that builds happy, constructive lives for all.

Botton Village is the cradle of relationship fundraising. The people who manage its fundraising are committed to a special way of life. Their material needs are taken care of from village funds, so they take no salaries, working unpaid seven days a week alongside the villagers, integral parts of one happy, productive community.

Donors find Botton irresistible, not just because of its charm but because it is disarmingly open and honest. Botton makes that perspective shift that seemed so vital to the Scottish poet Robbie Burns (see Chapter Two). The village's fundraisers are not playing at relationship marketing but genuinely want and seek to give their donors what they want.

It's this that most organizations find so hard to copy. Botton does things not to suit itself but because they're best for the donor. And over the years donors have responded happily to this—and very generously. Botton's fundraisers have always innovated in fundraising. Alongside rigorous testing they have pioneered new realms of segmentation. They scrapped checkboxes and requests for fixed amounts because they thought them patronizing and prescriptive.

They've always invited donors to visit the village, on a large scale. They were first to offer real choices to donors, letting them decide when and how Botton would communicate with them and about what. From the start they stressed accountability and sharp customer service.

They have as a result built a legion of remarkably sensitive, committed, and generous donors. Botton has been such a good fundraiser over the years that its fundraising needs are virtually fully met, so it can now stop asking.

It's my honor to visit Botton each year, to stroll around the village, awestruck at how it has developed, each step reminding me of the fruits of successful fundraising. When I first went there, Botton teetered on the verge of bankruptcy. Now the visitor sees a newly prosperous and thriving Botton.

Facing the visitor are the new creamery and bakery, behind them the splendid village hall and the award-winning church. Off to the right is the innovative special facility for elderly people with mental handicaps. Botton's households have been restored to standards as high as you'd find anywhere. The decay and despair that pervaded in 1983 have been replaced by buoyant, prosperous optimism. Evidence of what successful fundraising can achieve is all around.

Chapter Seven

WHAT'S NEXT?

13 Things That Will Be Coming Your Way

Fundraising is a complex and fast-changing profession. If you wish not just to keep up but to get and stay ahead, you'll have to work quite hard. And play clever.

77
Keeping ahead.

There are just a few sources of information for fundraisers that deserve to be described as required reading. These sources include all the books and Web sites listed here and a few of the leading journals that serve the sector. Internationally, the *International Journal of Nonprofit and Voluntary Sector Marketing* is highly regarded (if a tad expensive). In the UK, among the journals I like are *Third Sector* (www.thirdsector.co.uk) and *Professional Fundraising* (www.professionalfundraising.co.uk). In the United States, my list includes the *Chronicle of Philanthropy* (http://philanthropy.com), the *NonProfit Times* (www.nptimes.com), and *Contributions* magazine (www.contributions magazine.com). Serious fundraisers should consider subscribing to journals published in foreign lands—it's the quickest way to convincingly posture as an international expert.

78
Ten best books to keep by you.
Most of the following books are indispensable. Some are literally worth their weight in gold. Many fundraisers will have their own quite different lists of the Top Ten fundraising books, but this is my book, so here's my list (I have, at least, done the polite thing and listed my own books last):

Tiny Essentials of Fundraising, by Neil Sloggie (coupled with his follow-up, *Tiny Essentials of Major Gift Fundraising*)
Asking Properly, by George Smith
Revolution in the Mailbox, by Mal Warwick
Over Goal!, by Kay Sprinkel Grace
Hidden Gold, by Harvey McKinnon
Breakthrough Thinking, by Bernard Ross and Clare Segal
How to Write Successful Fundraising Letters, by Mal Warwick
How to Produce Inspiring Annual Reports, by Ken Burnett and Karen Weatherup
Friends for Life, by Ken Burnett
Relationship Fundraising, by Ken Burnett

79
Sites to see.
www.whitelionpress.com
www.burnettassociates.co.uk
www.lifetimevalue.co.uk
www.sofii.org

www.fundraisinguk.com
www.contributionsmagazine.com
www.professionalfundraising.co.uk
www.interscience.wiley.com/journal/nvsm
www.papilia.com
www.malwarwick.com
www.donorschoose.org
www.globalgiving.com
www.modestneeds.org
www.charityvillage.com
www.afpnet.org
www.institute-of-fundraising.org.uk
www.fia.org.au

80
Experience fundraising.

In the spirit of storytelling outlined in point 37 (in Chapter Three), fundraisers should aspire whenever possible to transport their donors directly to the cause so they can see it for themselves. For the best possible introduction to and immersion in a cause occurs when the donors can actually see, touch, feel, even smell the cause for themselves, in person. If your donors can be given such experiences, almost invariably they'll be yours for life.

The darkest hour is just before the dawn . . . so if you're going to steal your neighbor's newspaper, that's the time to do it.

But realistically, most of the time this won't be possible. So fundraisers have to do the next best thing, to learn the skill of taking the experience to their donors. This is when it pays to be a great storyteller, to be so good at it that you develop the facility to take donors, at the drop of a hat, directly to where the action is.

Donors must know what it's really like at the moment when equipment they've provided saves a child's life or when through research they've funded the mystery of a deadly disease is unraveled. They should be taken gently by the hand and led into the dark, squalid, mud and brick hut in rural Africa where a tiny undernourished child lies on the brink of death, wanting only a simple vaccine that donors can provide. They must be encouraged to sit, metaphorically, on the edge of a newly dug well that they've paid for, so they can hoist the first bucket of fresh, clear water, knowing that this well's longed-for arrival promises a regular, reliable supply of water that will transform life for a whole village. Donors must feel for themselves what it's like to place their lives on the line when they put their fragile, tiny boat between whalers armed with explosive harpoons and their helpless prey, the whale. They must know the fear that has to be overcome as they launch themselves into the teeth of a Force 9 gale and giant waves, thirty-foot foaming walls of water, at dead of night to rescue unknown sailors from a watery grave. They must sleep rough alongside the homeless on a cold night and take abandoned, unwanted pet dogs for a walk to give them and their rescue center a break. Donors must be given the chance to hold the hand of the father in his forties dying from cancer and to take tea with the young girl who has just completed a marathon without her legs.

OK, it sounds sentimental, even schmaltzy. But it isn't mawkish and it isn't out of place. By whatever means possible, fundraisers have to take the everyday experiences of their organization's work directly and personally to their donors to make the true impact of charitable giving come alive.

Our donors and supporters can't be there with us at times like the moment I describe in the next To Prove the Point story, about visiting a young man with AIDS. But we fundraisers are nothing if we are not communicators. It's the fundraiser's job to take donors along on such visits in words and pictures, to help them see the reality and why and how they should help. It is the fundraiser's job to inspire those donors, to show them that however hopeless things may seem, there is hope for a treatment, perhaps even for a cure. And if no cure is possible there is still the need for comfort, understanding, practical help, and trained support that will make it possible for people with this disease to bear the unbearable, to endure the unendurable.

We fundraisers have superb stories to tell, and we should use those stories better than we do. This demands that we spread inspiration, sharing our experiences to convey the real, painful, shattering, but ultimately optimistic and rewarding experience of helping other people in need.

This is experience fundraising.

TO PROVE THE POINT:
THE WORST TOURIST
IN THE WORLD

For five years, from 1998 to 2003, I was lucky enough to serve as chairman of trustees at ActionAid, Britain's third largest development aid agency. Along with much that was routine, even dull, my role had some privileges. A few years ago I was lucky enough to visit several African countries to

see ActionAid's work in the field of HIV/AIDS. My trip
included meeting people from partner organizations,
women's cooperatives, and groups living with HIV/AIDS.
These included some of the poorest and sickest people
on earth. I made lots of speeches and shook even more
hands.

Then, when I was in Zimbabwe, one of the people
ActionAid has trained to visit and support people living
with AIDS took me to the home of a young man who was
in the final stages of this utterly devastating disease.

He was just twenty-two years old, he had been
bedridden for four years, and he was clearly dying. I have
a son just a bit younger than him. But this young man's
home was nothing more than a shed. The floor was earth.
The bare walls of his dismal room were decorated only by
a single, crumpled photograph that showed the patient as
a fine young man in distant, much better days. An old
and dirty towel had been tacked across the window as a
makeshift curtain. A dilapidated cupboard was the only
furniture other than the creaking bed on which lay the
young man, in foul and sodden bedding. In the room with
him were his father, the ActionAid worker, and me.

For once I was utterly lost for words. I couldn't think
of anything to say in that room that would have had any
meaning or relevance whatsoever.

Then my guide asked me if I wanted to take a
photograph. And that was too much for me.

The thing is, I knew why the boy's father was there.
He was there to comfort and be with his dying son. I knew
why the ActionAid worker was there. She was there to offer

what was left of this family the meager support and help that she had been trained to give. And I knew why the young man was there. He was there because he had nowhere else to go. He was there to die from this disease called AIDS.

But at that moment I couldn't for the life of me imagine or explain why I was there. I felt like the worst kind of tourist. So without even a word of comfort for the others in that room, I left.

Of course I realized later that I was there for a reason. I was there because those people wanted to show me what dying of AIDS in Africa is really like. They wanted me to be there, they wanted me to see this death in its gut-wrenching awfulness, so I would tell others that we must do something to stop this. I was there because, as a fundraiser, it is my job to tell other people about situations exactly like this. If I hadn't seen it, I don't think I could ever have imagined it. So even though I found that meeting among the most uncomfortable of my life, and the hardest of events to come to terms with, because I was privileged to be there I have been able to tell many others about it and have, I hope, moved some of them to action.

81
Wish you were here.

Without doubt the best background from which to really inspire a donor is your having been on the spot and having seen for yourself something that matters.

For most of us, the only way we do experience fundraising convincingly is when we have the chance to see for ourselves, at first hand and in detail, the work that our non-profit does. Yet so many nonprofit employers skimp on sending their fundraisers to the front line. If they do it at all, fundraisers get to go only after they've been working for a cause for some time and often their visit will be restricted. It's the nonprofit that loses when fundraisers don't get to see these things themselves (and also, sadly, staff and donors too).

This has to change. Donors will believe fundraisers only when they can talk with the conviction of having been there and having seen for themselves.

82
Keep immaculate records for analysis and follow-up.

History, they say, is doomed forever to repeat itself because people are incapable of learning from experience. Don't let that be true for you. Because the world we live and work in is so complicated, we can't afford to trust to memory or rely on anecdotal information. Every fundraiser needs to keep accurate records so he or she isn't constantly condemned to repeat history.

Memory can be terrifyingly deceptive. How is it that we can't recall what we did the day before yesterday but can remember every word of the 1960s hit single "The Hippy, Hippy Shake," by the Swinging Blue Jeans?

A good database, of course, covers for such fallibilities of memory and is the keystone of anyone's relationship fundraising strategy. True one-to-one communication and relationship development are impossible without it. And beyond this, good, usable, and accessible records are essential if you are to continually appraise and improve your performance, to understand the impact of your testing and development program, and to feed knowledge into your annual communication cycle so your communications constantly get better and better.

Most people don't do this well, so if you can, it's another opportunity for you to get fifteen minutes ahead.

Over the years I've worked for several hundred different nonprofits in many parts of the world. I've lost count of the number of times nonprofits have been unable to answer my simple questions about their history because they don't keep decent archives. Many have poor, often only anecdotal information about their fundraising performance—what works and what doesn't. Many also can't easily lay their hands on this year's communications, far less the total communications of the last five years. Not keeping such useful, usable information is surely an expense, not a saving.

Every fundraiser should keep a *guard book* (so called because therein you guard your sacred research data), wherein are recorded all test results, advertising and direct-mail response data, and so forth and so on—in other words, proof of what works and what doesn't. Your guard book may be a computer-based system or a simple notebook, whatever suits you. It'll soon be more indispensable than your address book.

And when you leave your current employer to go on to pastures new, all the experience and learning from your most recent position will of course go with you. But a record of it will also stay where it belongs: in the guard book of the organization that paid for it.

83
Avoid the nonprofit
tendency to make false economies.

If donors hate waste, which is often less prevalent in nonprofits than they might imagine, they will for sure detest false economies, which in my experience abound among our employers. Their prevalence may just be part and parcel of the quirky nonprofit world, a symptom of the nature of this particular beast. But I think we should learn to spot false economies wherever they are and resist them at every turn, for they do much damage.

Nonprofits, it so often seems, would rather do the job on the cheap than do it well, would rather spend $50 and end up with little to show for it than spend $100 and get real value for money. This attitude is often promulgated by nonprofit boards, which frequently include among their ranks otherwise sensible and serious-minded businesspeople. These guys wouldn't dream of being so short-sighted with their own enterprises, but when they join a nonprofit board they appear to leave their brains behind in the car park. For even though the concepts of *speculate to accumulate* and *cheapest ain't necessarily best* are widely understood and accepted in the business world, in nonprofits they are normally notable for their absence.

Appreciation of the need to invest for the future is also still sadly rare in nonprofits. In particular one still frequently finds organizations with ample (often worryingly large) portfolios of investments in stocks and bonds, on which they too often get very little by way of growth and return, yet these same enterprises have barely invested enough in building their donor files, far less outlaid resources as necessary on a sensible program of donor relationship development.

We may hope that all this will change with the coming increased focus on good governance and improved understanding of what donors really want. But that will depend on fundraisers to lead the charge.

84
Take time to learn
what motivates your donors.

Sympathy, guilt, compassion, fellow feeling, anger, professional interest, personal connection . . . the decision to support a nonprofit may have been motivated by any one, or a combination, of these. Or by a lot of other things. My colleague Alan Clayton is managing director of the Cascaid Group, a marketing and communications company that has been analyzing nonprofit databases in the UK and getting amazing results from direct-mail appeals by sending different messages to a range of file segments; the choice of message is based on the motivations that have prompted or underpinned past giving behavior. Alan says, "We know that while one individual might give to a particular cause for a specific reason or reasons, others can give for entirely different reasons. As their relationship with an organization matures, these motives can be enhanced, added to, or can simply change. People will be more motivated to give if we can send them messages that meet their own needs and unique mix of motives" (*Professional Fundraising*, September 2003).

Cascaid uses a theoretical model and hard transactional data analysis to work out which message, or set of messages, is most likely to have spoken to what makes individual donors tick, what in their past giving has driven these donors to give, and what their needs are. Cascaid can then develop a segment communication plan that enables different donors to get the messages they want, how they want them, and when they want them—and the fundraiser gets higher value, more loyal and highly motivated donors.

Imagine for a moment all the different reasons why someone might give to your cause or organization. There are quite a lot, aren't there? Imagine knowing which of these motivations was most important to each of your donors and how this knowledge might enhance your fundraising results.

85
Communicate appropriately and effectively on the vital subject of legacies (bequests).

Bequests, also known as legacies, are the pot of gold at the end of the fundraiser's rainbow. But it's important to get your thinking right about legacies. If you do, the benefits are obvious—in the UK, about one-third of all voluntary income comes in the form of bequests. (This ratio is probably similar in other countries, but statistics are often unreliable or unavailable.) But if your thinking about bequests is wrong, the damage you can do to donor relationships is considerable.

Bequest fundraising is the art of building whole relationships. Our slogan here should be, "A bequest? Leave it to your donor, and your donor will leave it to you."

If people feel connected to your organization, are interested by it, inspired by it, trust and like it, then they will be loyal to it. This means they will support the organization faithfully over the years, will contribute to it as they think appropriate, and if asked properly (in the right way, by the right person, at the right time, and in the right format), they will agree to leave a bequest in their will.

The bequest is not a product that should be thought of or promoted in isolation. The bequest message should gently pervade everything your organization does. It will not be in any way a hard sell. On the contrary it should come across to donors as very natural and expected, no surprise at all. In time donors will understand and accept almost without thinking that a bequest is one of the foremost and best ways through which they'll choose to support your organization.

You shouldn't be in a rush to promote your bequest strategy. Rather you should take time to communicate effectively about bequests and to explain to supporters the paramount importance of supporting the organization in this way.

TO PROVE THE POINT: BEQUEST MARKETING WAS A MISTAKE

In my time as a fundraiser I've made lots of mistakes. One of my biggest, and with hindsight most obvious and most avoidable, occurred when, many years ago, I espoused and evangelized for the then virtually unknown practice of bequest (legacy) marketing. I really regret that now. I'm talking here not about marketing as a theoretical, academic subject but as it is practiced day in day out by today's nonprofits.

It's not that I no longer believe bequest marketing works. It does. I have experiences that prove it. But then, just talking about bequests works. Printing "We depend on bequests" as part of your letterhead works. Telling your supporters in your newsletters and face-to-face about how much your nonprofit has achieved thanks to bequest X and bequest Y will also, eventually, work rather well. Consistently and positively making the case for bequests at every appropriate opportunity will work too, often spectacularly and probably at an impressively low cost to income ratio. The promotion of charitable bequests may take longer to reach fruition than most other forms of commercial undertaking, but there is no doubt that bequests can be successfully promoted by those with a little skill, some politeness and savoir faire, and reasonable amounts of commitment and patience.

But the question is, *How* should bequests be promoted? For though bequest marketing may indeed work, it may be unwise. As I've said, donors don't want to be marketed at. They never have done. They particularly don't welcome a nonprofit *selling* them the concept of leaving money to that nonprofit after their death. And those qualities I just listed as important to the successful promotion of bequests are, sadly, usually absent in bequest marketing and the people who practice it.

Rather obviously, persuading someone to leave your organization a bequest—or even suggesting or gently hinting that someone should do so—is something that should be done with great delicacy and sensitivity. My favorite example of how this task can go painfully awry in the hands of marketing types comes from the early days of bequest marketing, when a major British charity wrote to its donors with, emblazoned on the outer envelope, the starkly poignant message, "DO YOU BELIEVE IN LIFE AFTER DEATH?" The example I saw of this pack, addressed to a Mrs. Crosby, had been returned to the nonprofit simply marked "deceased." Mrs. Crosby, I guess, could have answered the question. But I doubt she did.

Surprisingly, though my wife and I support more than a few charities, only one that I can think of has written to us recently on the "b" subject. And that letter was fairly inoffensive and instantly forgettable. Indeed most bequest promotions I've seen, particularly those sent through the mail, have been more bland than offensive and as such are often indistinguishable from the regular stream of asking that floods the average donor's mailbox. As the bulk of bequest marketing fails to inspire or even to stand out from the less long-term appeals that surround it, it's reasonable to assume that bequest missives generally share the fate of most fundraising communication. That is, they will find acceptance if not quite favor with a tiny minority while offending some, irritating more than a few, and eliciting indifference from the majority (thereby finding their way swiftly into the wastebasket, often unopened).

But bequests are nonprofits' lowest-cost, highest-potential source of voluntary income. So how should we promote the idea of leaving our nonprofit a bequest? The answer will be found only in a deep analysis of donors' motivations, desires, and interests and a keen understanding of why they might decide to leave a bequest to a particular organization. At the end of a lifetime (or perhaps less) of donating to your cause, perhaps just in a small way, why would any of your donors choose to leave a truly major gift to this cause that they've supported, loved, and believed in?

I wonder . . . does this seem like something we can readily sell by direct mail? Only if we're really, really good, I would submit. Only if we can write copy that will make a donor's heart soar.

It may be sad, but it's undeniably true. The key to success in bequest promotion, as in all forms of fundraising, is to realize that ours is nothing less than the inspiration business. For we shouldn't just ask for money; we must inspire it. In no arena of fundraising is this more true than in the raising of bequests.

It seems that as our job of raising money gets more and more difficult, we fundraisers find ourselves having to stoop ever lower to raise it. That doesn't seem very desirable or sustainable to me.

That's why I say marketing was a mistake, and not just for the bequest fundraiser but for all fundraisers. We should switch the current fundraising as marketing paradigm to a new fundraising as communication paradigm. And we should embrace the communications revolution that, thanks to a new attitude and the advent of some spectacular new technology, will very soon be coming our way.

86
Encourage *real* donor involvement in your organization.

I said earlier that we should offer donors the chance to become actively involved in our organizations. This will pay. Here are some ideas for how to do it:

- Provide quality donor experiences that show donors what their dollars (or pounds, euros, or whatever) are achieving.
- Make it possible for different departments to work together to make donor participation possible—for instance, the campaign, program, and communications departments.

- Take donors on trips or project visits; they will contribute much more significantly to work they have seen for themselves, and they will be more loyal and better advocates.

- Offer incentives to donors and staff that are mission related.
- Allow donors to interact with each other.
- Organize cultivation events and also celebration events, where there's no immediate ask for money.

If you ever think that you are too small to make a difference . . . you've never spent the night alone in a room with a mosquito.

- Set up pivotal relationships with key donor groups who can influence lots of others — for instance, teachers, media experts, broadcasters, and so forth.

87
Outlaw killer phrases in your organization.

Here are some examples:

"That won't work."
"We can't afford it."
"It's never been done before."
"Let's form a committee."
"Here we go again!"
"We're not ready."
"There isn't time."
"Our donors won't like it."

You just don't have time to indulge such attitudes.

88
We must take advantage of the progress paradox.

The world is changing fast. Some of the consequences of this are surprising and will open up opportunities hitherto not even guessed at for those who would fundraise. Massive social upheavals that are already starting may lead to as yet undreamed of chances for the nonprofit sector. But as with all opportunities we have to spot them in time and exploit them to the full.

Progress, it seems, isn't necessarily making the human species happier. These days Western society's unease may not be coming, as it traditionally has, from endemic poverty, from people having to go without, so much as from prosperity, people being increasingly able to go *with*. General affluence, it appears, does not automatically come in the company of general contentment. It's in the most affluent of societies that one finds the longest queues outside the psychiatrists' offices.

According to Robert Samuelson, writing in *Newsweek* (March 22, 2004), as living standards improve, people don't necessarily feel the benefits. Although folks now are starting work later in life and retiring earlier and in reality have oodles more discretionary time than their ancestors did, they feel time poor. Obesity is now as large a health risk for the affluent as going hungry is for the poor. And, like poverty, it's growing. Instead of more money making people happier, griping apparently rises with income.

More and more people, it seems, find that with increasing affluence comes a decreasing sense of fulfillment. Maybe as people cease to need to worry about basic survival, other issues of purpose and fulfillment crowd in on them.

Look! We offer meaning . . .

Could this be an opportunity for the likes of us? I think so, and it could be a great one. Perhaps in this new progress paradigm, nonprofits can expand their role. If fulfillment is moving up in people's hierarchies of basic needs, where better could they turn to find what's lacking in their lives than to the nonprofit sector? If their problems stem from their growing affluence, maybe we're just the folks to relieve them of it. If the meaning of life is becoming increasingly incomprehensible, cannot fundraisers and the causes they work for help many people find the answers they seek?

Think about it.

 ## TO PROVE THE POINT: CAN YOU SPARE THE TIME TO CHANGE THE WORLD?

I wonder if, like me, you sometimes feel this modern world is going just too fast? Perhaps, as I am, you're increasingly coming to doubt that the many technological advances of our times are actually making our lives easier and better, as they promised they would? By any chance, does your daily e-mail mountain also seem to you ever harder to climb and less interesting to boot, as mine does? Or does it trouble you, as it does me, that while you can now be reached by telephone pretty much wherever you happen to be, this additional intrusion hasn't really made you more effective, more efficient, or more importantly, happier, as it should have done?

If any of the above doubts apply, you're not alone. I suspect a lot of us share them and with good reason. They've hit me particularly hard because I've chosen a lifestyle somewhat different from most.

I've lived in rural France for eleven years now, while most of my clients, colleagues, and business contacts live in other lands (mainly in and around London). In the early days of this self-imposed separation I used to secretly revel in my newly limited availability, in people's reluctance to disturb me with an international call, in the fact that my attendance at meetings was an added bonus rather than the accepted norm.

The invisible, imaginary line that was implied by my physical distance meant that I could spend time with my wife and kids while others were working, which I loved. Or I could take my dogs for long walks in the early mornings while my colleagues endured commutes by subway, bus, and train to their daily grind or wrestled with technology that hadn't quite caught up with me yet. Some years back I visited the Greenpeace office in Washington, D.C., with its international director of fundraising, who was from Amsterdam. He had thirteen e-mails waiting while I, an e-mail virgin, had none. So while he toiled indoors I was sent for a long walk outside. It was cherry blossom time in D.C. then—lovely!

Then in rapid succession to my French fortress came e-mail, the Internet, mobile phones, and lower call charges. And conference calls. And FedEx and DHL. And I suppose, this society's increasing familiarity and ease with modern technology, matched by a growing impatience that means nothing can be waited for, gratification has to be instant, responses have to be now or next day at the latest. From these miracles of modern communication there is no escape, for in these busy, competitive times everything is a race against the clock.

It seems there's no escape, as yet. But a means may be coming. Fundraisers who feel particularly burdened or cursed by the go-faster society should read a book called *In Praise of Slow,* by Carl Honoré (Orion Press, 2004). Carl has set himself on a mission against the cult of speed. He promotes what he claims is rapidly becoming a worldwide movement: the campaign for slow, which advocates among other things slow food; a better life-work balance; more green spaces, pedestrian-only zones, and areas devoted to calm and tranquillity; and taking time to read proper bedtime stories to your kids. Carl thinks the trend toward calm will catch on—slowly (the slow-food campaign now apparently has 78,000 members in fifty countries).

But is the rush of modern life a reality or just an illusion, a media-fuelled misunderstanding? The truth is, most people really don't need more time. Modern men and women enjoy more leisure time these days than ever before, yet somehow everyone imagines the opposite. Something in modern lives appears to compel people to cram in as much experience and consumption as possible, in the misguided notion that this is how they will add meaning and fulfillment to their increasingly empty lives.

Here's another thought. Does this possible misconception, this progress paradox, perhaps present just the kind of opportunity that today's fundraisers should be grabbing eagerly with both hands?

What could be more appropriate for affluent people in a hurry than an appropriately crafted proposition from fundraisers who can make it easy for these people to find useful, worthwhile, and interesting homes for their excess money, without any pressure, fuss, hassle, or onerous time commitment? We could soon build for ourselves a reputation as *the* people to turn to when the pressures of modern affluence become too much to bear.

This role as provider of fulfillment for busy people on the move might be a better role for the fundraiser than that which he or she currently enjoys.

89
What goes around, comes around.

What will be the next big thing in donor acquisition? Possibly it will plummet into nonviability as the grubby marketing practices of most fundraisers so taint our collective image that no decent, upright individual will ever think of publicly admitting to support for our cause. Or, we can hope, fundraisers of the future will realize that they won't have a future unless they can better communicate their complex but moving and engaging messages. If they can do this creatively, then it won't be necessary for them to solicit support, because donors will beat a path to their door.

However, it seems unlikely that any day soon most fundraisers will stop acquiring new donors solely because they are finding the process too expensive. So the search for the next big medium of donor recruitment—a means of finding and involving new donors in sufficient volume at acceptable cost—will surely continue.

- Direct mail will almost certainly remain a staple recruitment and communication method for the foreseeable future. But we'll have to get much better at it and at other forms of direct response promotion so that donors in the future will both welcome it and find it engaging.

- Press, or off-the-page, advertising (where readers respond by returning a card or coupon), currently being rested by many fundraisers, may return.
- Loose inserts, scourge of the quality Sunday newspapers, might also make a comeback, for a while.
- One-on-one (or face-to-face or street) fundraising has made a strong comeback in many countries. When I was a fundraiser, about a quarter of a century ago, I scrapped this in my organization, to make room for the then new god, direct mail. But in 1994, my colleague George Smith and I helped introduce monthly giving and legacy promotion to Greenpeace offices in sixteen countries. Shortly afterward Greenpeace Austria was signing up new donors in the street for automated monthly payments. The rest, as they say, is economics . . .
- Fundraisers will make much better use than hitherto of the new electronic media, particularly e-mail and the Internet. I can't see texting as a primary means of recruitment, though I welcome its use in supportive roles. (But hey, I've been wrong before . . .)
- What could be new? Giving circles or giving groups, perhaps (see Chapter One)? Blackmail? Or mass abductions? Interactive television? The ozone layer? Semaphore? Or . . . ?

Here I'll defer to what has become for me something of a hobbyhorse—my view that the best form of acquisition is retention.

I've reached this conclusion after contemplating the major dilemma that currently afflicts fundraisers—what to do about the 50 or more percent of expensively acquired new donors who stop giving after their first gift or in their first year because, presumably, we've failed to reach them, or at least to inspire them, with an offer, proposition, or enticement sufficiently compelling to convince them to keep supporting the world-changing work that we do. Yet a certain UK insurance company—a mere commercial peddler of financial service products—reportedly gets 95 percent of its new business through referrals from happy customers.

Why can't the nonprofit sector achieve something close to this? Why are the majority of our customers, our donors, not advocates or even evangelists for our cause, bringing in as supporters (at no acquisition cost) their friends, family, colleagues, and contacts in droves because they find supporting us such a worthwhile thing to do and dealing with us such a treat?

That is the challenge facing fundraisers now. Our industry needs a complete change in the way it is seen by its publics. To achieve this, we have first to change ourselves. That means getting very much better at what this book is all about, enhancing the experiences of our volunteer customers, our donors.

As I said earlier, it's not rocket science. It shouldn't be too difficult. And we don't have to don hair shirts or sacrifice our lifestyles to achieve it. I cling to the belief that it's possible to save the world and still be in the pub by 5:30.

We just need to believe in what we're doing, know how we should go about it, and put it into practice. These eighty-nine points are here to help you do just that. Good luck!

ACKNOWLEDGMENTS

When It Comes to Saying Thank You, This Book Practices What It Preaches

Wonderful Vhen, having been at the receiving end of great generosity, Scottish people say, "I'll be forever in your debt," they usually mean, "There is no possibility whatsoever that I will ever pay you back." By publicly posting these acknowledgments, this particular Scotsman wishes to make an exception. Well, true, no money may change hands, but at least the sentiment of appreciation is sincere.

Acknowledgments is just a fancy way of saying, "I am truly grateful to you; I'm in your debt." A lot of people have helped me with this book. Although I probably won't remember everyone, I'd like to say a special thank you to Chuck Longfield of Target Software, Inc., in the USA, Alan Clayton and Roger Lawson of Cascaid Marketing, in the UK, and Sean Triner of Pareto Fundraising, in Australia, for surveying the final manuscript and making sure all major gaffs and omissions have been rectified prior to printing. For their inspiration I'd also like to thank Bernard Ross, Harvey McKinnon, Beth Isokoff, Dick McPherson, Nick Allen, Karin Weatherup, David Brann, John Grain, Paul McFadden, Jerry Cianciolo, Giles Pegram, and Tom Ahern.

I'm grateful to several fundraisers whose commitment to accountability and to thanking donors has inspired me and informed my approach to the thank-you process. They include David Love and Gwen Chapman (whom I met through WWF Canada) and Penelope Burk, whose book *Donor-Centered Fundraising* is required reading for any serious relationship fundraiser.

I'm grateful too to my editor at Jossey-Bass, Allison Brunner, and to senior editor Dorothy Hearst for their helpful and insightful comments and guidance on both content and structure, coupled with warm support for this project from the outset. And sincere thanks to senior production editor Xenia Lisanevitch and my razor-sharp copyeditor Elspeth MacHattie. Your tolerance is appreciated, believe me.

And most of all I'd like to thank my editor-in-chief, Marie Burnett, who apart from sharing my life in other more conventional ways has been checking my proofs and covering up for my mistakes and shortcomings for the last three decades or more. As with everything else she does she just gets better and better at it.

Some of the stories under the heading "To Prove the Point" are derived from various articles I have had published over the past three or four years as regular columns in the U.S. journal *Contributions* and in the U.K. magazine *Professional Fundraising*. A full list of my articles can be accessed on my Web site, www.whitelionpress.com.

Finally, much of this book is my original thinking, but some of the thoughts, concepts, and ideas herein are adapted, absorbed by osmosis, or in some way or another borrowed from others, and for this I thank these others unreservedly.

Whenever I've known of a specific source I've sought to identify and acknowledge it, as I hope others will do with my stuff. But, like most authors, I recognize that's not always possible. Although I'm not sure of their exact origins, the Zen sayings have enlivened a number of my seminars over the years. As with several of my observations on the science and art of fundraising, though I may have embroidered and embellished them I didn't invent them in the first place. To those whose thoughts, sayings, or actions I have learned from over the years and have recycled so others may benefit too, I trust you will agree that plagiarism is the most sincere form of flattery.

—*K. B.*

About the Author

In 1992, a book came out in Britain that some said, "changed forever the way fundraisers think about and treat their donors." *Relationship Fundraising: A Donor-Based Approach to the Business of Raising Money* soon gained an enthusiastic following among fundraisers all over the world. In 2002, after three printings, the publisher of the book you're now reading, Jossey-Bass, brought out a second, fully revised edition of the now classic *Relationship Fundraising*. This updated edition is rooted in the twenty-nine-year fundraising experience of one of the UK's best-known fundraising and communications specialists, Ken Burnett.

Almost a decade and a half after its first appearance, *Relationship Fundraising* is selling more copies than it ever did (though, sadly, not yet enough to encourage its author to give up his day job; total sales after thirteen years are about as many as J. K. Rowling sells of *Harry Potter* in maybe thirteen minutes. Though we could be fooling ourselves here. They're probably much less).

Recently the UK trade magazine *Professional Fundraising* ran an article attempting to identify future fundraising gurus under the headline, "The next Ken Burnett." Somewhat embarrassed, Ken responded that he was having enough difficulty being the current Ken Burnett: "Anyone who wants to be the next one is welcome to it."

If you would like to find out more about Ken Burnett, please visit www.kenburnett.com and www.whitelionpress.com. You can contact him via e-mail at ken@kenburnett.com.